Trophy Blacktails:
The Science of the Hunt

Trophy Blacktails:
The Science of the Hunt
By Scott Haugen

H·E

Haugen, Scott

First Edition

Haugen Enterprises
2009, Springfield, OR

Softbound ISBN: 978-0-9819423-0-8

Photography by Scott Haugen
www.scotthaugen.com

Book Design & Cover by Media Contractors, Inc.
www.MediaContractors.com

Printed in Singapore

Dedication

To my favorite hunting partners: My dad, Jerry Haugen, for introducing me into the great sport of blacktail deer hunting; my wife Tiffany, whom I never get to spend enough time with; and my sons, Braxton and Kazden, who I now have the honor of taking into the woods and keeping the dream alive, for all of us.

Acknowledgments

Motivation is a big reason why we do things in life. Hunting black-tail deer is no different. For most hunters motivation is self-induced. The drive to achieve comes from within our hearts. The same was true for me, until I started making my living in the outdoors.

Since undertaking a blessed, full-time outdoor career beginning in 2001, sharing my experiences with fellow hunters has become one of my greatest rewards in life. Be it through television shows, magazine articles, radio broadcasts, books or sport show seminars, sharing information that helps sportsmen find success, means I'm doing my job the way I've envisioned.

For me, self-motivation is still a driving force to my blacktail deer hunting addiction, but I also have the support and encouragement of you, my fellow hunter. Were it not for your interest in wanting to become a better blacktail deer hunter, this book would have never taken form.

Throughout the course of any given year, I have the good fortune of meeting many sportsmen. Because most of my time and hunting efforts are spent in the West, that's where most conversations gravitate. And of all the great species we have to hunt and talk about in the West, the majority of conversations lead to what many consider to be the most challenging of all big game, the Columbia blacktail deer.

For all who aspire to become accomplished blacktail deer hunters, this book is for you. For those who have more secrets than what I've unveiled, I hope there's at least some information found within these pages that will help to put your tags on more trophy blacktail bucks.

To everyone reading this book, thank you for the motivation you've provided me which drives me to become a better blacktail deer hunter, and share what I've learned.

Safe hunting and God bless,

Scott Haugen

Contents

Foreword

Growing up in California I cut my teeth hunting blacktail deer. Boy, did they give me the fits! It wasn't until college that I began traveling to other states to seriously hunt the more glamorous mule deer. Once I did, I remember thinking, "Compared to the blacktail back home, these things are dumber than a box of rocks!"

Of course there was a lot of information available to help a mule deer hunter back in the 1960s and '70s in the form of magazine articles and books. If you were a blacktail hunter, though, you relied on yourself and, if you were lucky, an experienced mentor, to help you. It was not until later that a very few books and videos appeared. All of them helped, but all left me feeling like there was something missing.

Until now!

Scott Haugen has finally written the definitive book on blacktail hunting. It's not based on myth or the experiences of a few hunts taken on private land where the deer are tame, but on a lifetime of hunting them on his own, on public land throughout their range, from California to Alaska. Forget the fact that Scott – a native Oregonian whose family has hunted blacktail since the 1880s – has lived and hunted big game in several countries around the world, in some of the wildest environments on the planet. Scott has a master's degree and a biology background, and combines these experiences with more than 30 years of hunting blacktail deer on heavily-hunted public lands where even young bucks have graduate degrees in hunter behavior.

This book doesn't fill its pages with information you can find in a few hours on the internet or in the various record books. The book's value is in the lessons taught by a man who has never done things the easy way. Throughout the book, Scott highlights his points with personal anecdotes of what he has observed and learned over the years, providing a real feel for what's happening out there, today, in the same places you go hunting.

In this book Scott breaks down the six different habitats of Columbia blacktails, plus the two different habitats of the Sitka deer. He then looks at their behaviors based on where they live, analyzing their routines and the science of their day-to-day lives, including what they eat and how they communicate, and how hunters can scout and hunt these different ecosystems, doing things year-round to improve overall success.

In the world of outdoor writers, there are just a handful that I classify as the "Real Deal." These are the guys who do the majority of their hunting the hard way, who still hunt on their own regardless of their position. They are also the ones who are fit enough to climb the tallest mountain, skilled enough with rifle, bow and muzzleloader to make the toughest shot, time and time again, who know how to make it happen in the woods even when the odds are long and conditions less than ideal, who never, ever give up no matter how tough the going gets. Scott Haugen is such a man. He doesn't have to make it up, because he has been there, done that.

Whether you are an experienced blacktail hunter or just getting started, this book's lessons are invaluable. It should be a part of every serious blacktail hunter's arsenal.

– Bob Robb

Introduction:
Columbia Blacktails,
The Ultimate Skill-Builder

Give me a person who was raised hunting the Columbia blacktail deer, and who can consistently take trophy bucks, and I'll show you a person who is likely competent enough to hunt just about any big game animal on the planet.

It's a strong statement, I know, but one I wholeheartedly believe in. I feel it's true because I was raised in the heart of some of the best blacktail hunting land there is – the western foothills of Oregon's Cascade Range – and these animals taught me how to hunt. I've been very fortunate to travel much of the planet and hunt for some of the world's most prized big game animals. What I've concluded regarding many of those animals I've successfully hunted, like Africa's dangerous game and many coveted deer of the South Pacific, is that getting there is the primary difficulty. Though they are exciting animals to hunt, they don't regularly demand the all-around skill that the Columbia blacktail requires.

At the same time, I've faced the physical rigors of sheep, mountain goat and elk hunting, and know that pursuing high-country blacktails helped prepare me for such hunts, in multiple ways. I've also faced and taken each of North America's bears, and the drive that pushed me to the next level on these demanding hunts stemmed from the early education I received hunting blacktail deer.

For me, like many whom live west of the Cascade Mountains, the Columbia blacktail is a part of my culture. Both of my grandfathers started hunting these deer prior to 1950. On my wife's side of the family, blacktail hunting dates even further back, well into the 1800s.

Today, both my wife and I are honored to be raising our two sons, Braxton and Kazden, where we grew up in Walterville, Oregon. This is in the heart of Lane County, one of the top blacktail regions in the world. There are many reasons why we choose to live where we do, and as expected, one of those has to do with the fact we can teach our boys how to hunt using the blacktail woods as a classroom.

Blacktail deer are unlike any other deer species I've hunted in North America. The only other animals I've found that come close, both in behavior and habitat, are the elusive sambar deer of Australia and New Zealand, and the much sought after sika deer of the north island of New Zealand. In Africa, it's the bushbuck which always reminds me of blacktails, for they possess so many of the same behaviors in similar, brushy terrain.

The Haugen's have been hunting blacktails for several generations. These three bucks are the result of one day's efforts, taken back in the 1960s.

So what is it that makes blacktail deer so difficult to hunt? And what do they teach us, both as hunters and as people? That's precisely the objective of this book, to unlock the science behind what makes these deer so elusive, so tough to consistently attain.

Blacktail deer hunting takes place in a wide range of habitats, all of which require special skills and know-how in order to put a trophy on the ground. In the Coast Range of California, Oregon, Washington and British Columbia, rugged terrain combines with dense, jungle-like habitat to create what could be the most challenging of all blacktail hunting grounds.

Moving inland, the valley floors offer yet another variation of blacktail habitat. Though the land here is easy to traverse, the big bucks that live and die here could well be the wisest of all.

Stepping into the foothills of the Cascade Range, brush-choked timber dominates the blacktail's world, offering hunters a lifetime of challenge. Here, both resident and migratory hunts can be had, with seasons starting in late summer and in some areas, extending into December. With such a range of seasons, elevation and habitat, effecting deer behavior, many consider this the toughest area to score trophy bucks.

Progressing into the high country, increased elevation, bigger timber, and rough terrain throw yet another type of challenge at the blacktail deer hunter. Here, early season hunts can be very productive, yet late in the season, when these deer begin their annual migration, hunting them transforms into a different game. These are the reasons so many hunters rate the high-country blacktails among the most challenging to hunt.

Given the wide range of habitats Columbia blacktail deer call home, it's easy to see why the hunter requires such an array of hunting skills. Include the fact that big bucks turn nocturnal almost immediately after shedding their velvet, and become even more secretive once the pressure of hunting season kicks-in, and it's hard to believe any big bucks are killed. But they are, every year.

Successful blacktail deer hunting comes down to knowing the biology of the animals, the habitat in which they live, their cyclical behavior patterns based on breading season and changing photoperiods, and finally, how we choose to pursue them. To successfully hunt these deer year after year, a complete understanding of their life-cycle and overall behavior is a necessity. That's the purpose of this book, to reveal precisely that information.

How I hunt an early season buck in velvet, high in the Cascades, is far different from how I'll go after them in the middle of October at lower elevations. How I stealth through the tangled mess of brush along the coastal mountains is not the same way I choose to still-hunt in more open land. How I glass in big timbered country early in the season is not how I glass later in the season, when the deer start behaving and moving differently. And how I track big bucks in lowland habitats is not the same way I go about it in the high country, for the deer have different agendas and places in which they carry them out.

I've been fortunate to hunt blacktails throughout their range, and take them with bow, rifle, muzzleloader and shotgun. My family and I have taken dozens of record book bucks over the years, too, but personally I've never entered them in any type of record book. Though I thrive on hunting big blacktail bucks, entering them into record books is something that's never been a personal, motivating factor as to why I hunt them.

The focus of this book is on blacktail deer behavior and how hunters can bring all the elements together to find success, no matter what time of year they hunt or what weapon they choose to use. We'll look closely at deer behavior for every given part of the year, and build hunting scenarios around that. This is the science of blacktail deer hunting as I know it, and it all began when I took my first buck, a 4-point, at the age of 12, in 1976.

I'll never forget my first blacktail hunt which took place in the foothills of Oregon's Cascades, not far from our Walterville home. It was opening day of the general rifle season, on public land. Dad and I took off early, and situated ourselves on the edge of a logged unit, hoping to catch a buck as it fed into the timber. What we found were two nice bucks, and Dad let me have first crack. My shot connected, the buck went down. My grandmother, Vi Lupon, was also with us, which made the experience that much sweeter. Grandma was a blacktail hunter and took a few great bucks over the years.

Actually, my blacktail education began well before killing my first deer. At the age of two, both my father and grandfathers would carry me into the blacktail woods, planting a seed of passion which has lasted a lifetime. Were it not for them introducing me to the mysterious world of the blacktail at such an early age, I'm certain my passion for hunting these grand deer would not run as deep.

Today, both of my grandfathers have passed away, but not without having left a solid impression of blacktail hunting on me. In fact, my

Grandpa Lupon died while hunting blacktails, suffering a heart attack on the very stump from which he'd taken many big bucks over his years of hunting.

I've been fortunate to see so much of the world and hunt so many of its glorious creatures. My wife and I have lived in Alaska's Arctic and in the jungle of Sumatra, Indonesia. We could live and raise our family anywhere we choose. We choose to do so where we grew up. Part of our reasoning has to do with family. Other parts have to do with all the great adventures this place has to offer, not the least of which is the fact that we're in blacktail country.

By the end of this book, you'll learn a great deal about the Columbia blacktail deer, and understand why my passion for hunting them is so strong, and hopefully, so contagious. You'll also learn about the Sitka blacktail, for this deer can be every bit as exciting to hunt as its Columbian cousin.

Chapter One
Meet the Blacktails

The Columbia blacktail deer is an elusive creature that tests the skills of big game hunters like no other animal I know in North America. Combine the wise characteristics of a whitetail deer with the sharp-eyed, alert instincts of a mule deer, toss it into an elk's habitat and you get the most evasive deer of all, the blacktail.

In this chapter we'll take a close look at the types of black-tailed deer, where they live, and their life-cycle. By gaining insight into the biology of these deer, you'll come away with a more thorough understanding of how blacktails live, what they depend on for survival and what environmental factors influence their behavior. That's just a sampling of the important scientific-based aspects to be learned about these deer, and all with the intent to help hunters become more successful.

Keep in mind, that while some of the following blacktail classifications have been instilled by various national and regional record books, others are based on my own personal opinion. My classifications are based solely on deer behavior, how their lives are carried out in respective habitats, and to some extent, physical characteristics. I think this section is one of the most important of the entire book, for it defines specific blacktail populations that will help give hunters a complete understanding of what they are up against.

I think one of the biggest mistakes hunters make is when they try to generalize blacktail behavior, and assume all bucks behave in the same way. From what I've found, there is no such thing as a typical blacktail buck. Bucks act differently from one another, even if they're of the same age class living in the same area. Their lifestyles can be different on a year-round basis, even during the rut.

Rather than trying to encapsulate blacktail behaviors into one nice little package, accept the fact that not all deer are the same. The blacktail deer, especially the trophy bucks, have many faces.

The Many Faces of Blacktails

Based on my experiences, I feel there are six different faces of the Columbia blacktail deer and two of the Sitka blacktail deer. For the Columbia blacktails you get bucks living in the highest elevations, what I call Cascade blacktails. Dropping in elevation you find bucks living in the foothills of the Cascades, what I call foothill blacktails, followed by valley floor blacktails, coastal blacktails, open country blacktails and finally, the high country blacktails of California. For the Sitka blacktails, I split these into what I call alpine deer and forest deer. Mind you, genetically speaking, scientists only recognize one strain of Columbia blacktail and one strain of Sitka blacktail, but when it comes to hunting, based on habitat and deer behavior, I think the blacktail puzzle is much more complex. Let's take a look at each of these blacktail subgroups.

The Columbia blacktail deer, *Odocoileus hemionus columbianus*, can be found along the Pacific coastal mountain region and into the Cascade Mountain Range from California to British Columbia. Because their habitat is so diverse, there is a wide range of behavioral characteristics that these deer display in order to survive and reproduce.

Some serious blacktail hunters, who have pursued them in all of their respective habitats and know blacktails inside and out, feel there should be a separate subcategory for each in the record books. If you've ever hunted blacktails in the thick coastal habit, on valley floors and high in the Cascades, you can understand where their reasoning comes from. Each of these deer live in different habitats and their behaviors are unique to suit their lifestyle.

A seasoned blacktail hunter will even be able look at the racks of various deer and tell you the general region the buck came from. A prime example is the comparison of short, stocky-framed coastal bucks,

Blacktail deer occupy a wide range of habitats, and getting to know each one is important to hunting success.

with the wide and sometimes spindly racks of deer that have come from open country.

With that in mind, let's take a closer look at the Columbia blacktail and the variety of habitats it calls home. We'll start in the high elevation ranges and work toward the coast.

Starting in the Cascade Range of the northwest and extending into the Sierra Nevada Range in California, you'll find blacktails living at surprisingly high elevations. No matter what you call these bucks, *Cascade blacktails*, benchlegs or inland blacktails, the fact that they are capable of crossbreeding with mule deer is what sets them apart from other blacktails.

Some record books do recognize these deer as a unique subspecies among blacktails, and have separate categories for listing them. Many hunters consider this subspecies to be the most beautifully marked of all blacktails. These mountain-dwelling bucks often carry distinct coloration on their hides, with white throat patches that bear a strong contrast to the often darker browns, blacks and deep grays on the rest of the neck and head.

The antler configuration of the Cascade deer can also vary. This is due to genetics and also the fact that they will cross with mule deer. Often these racks are more like mule deer in appearance, with wider, sweeping frames that don't carry the mass like brush country blacktails.

Then again, a buck may come from the 6,000-foot elevation mark that is 100% blacktail, or at least appears to be. At the same time, there are mule deer hunters who are taking bucks on the east side of the mountains that look more like blacktails than muleys. This is because the deer do crossbreed and migrate off both sides of the Cascades. The fact these deer can, but don't always, breed with muleys is too bad, because I think there are some monster, pure-strain blacktails taken each year in these higher elevations that don't get recognized as such.

Cascade blacktail hunts can take place in some of the West's most rugged terrain, at elevations up to 6,000-feet, even higher. These are deer that live at high elevations throughout the spring, summer and early fall, then migrate to lower elevations with winter's onset.

Early season Cascade blacktail hunts are among the best of all, for the simple reason bucks can still be in velvet, (depending on the hunting season) which makes them easier to spot since they are still in the open. Hunters who are willing to explore areas removed from well traveled logging roads and widely used hiking trails will routinely find the best bucks. Be in good shape and ready to cover ground. As the season progresses, hunting becomes tough until the rut or migration kicks in. Often these bucks will start cruising for does earlier than other blacktails, meaning hunters will want to start hitting it hard around October 21st or 22nd, depending on the season.

Be ready to glass, walk, and glass some more. Due to the rugged nature of this hunt, be prepared to pack animals out a long way. Late in the season, calling and rattling can be highly effective, especially if the rut coincides with the migration. Studies in the state of Washington have found migratory blacktails to move more than 17 miles from

4

**The Cascade Range is big, rugged country, and
home to a number of migratory blacktails.**

summer to wintering grounds. Southern Oregon's and northern
California's inland blacktails also undergo impressive seasonal migrations.

Some record books delineate the range of Cascade blacktails based
on segregation by major highway divisions, mountain ranges, and river
drainages. Generally speaking, the cutoff point that I personally use
for the Cascade deer's range in the areas I've hunted, based on deer
behavior and their yearly lifestyles, is around the 1,500 foot elevation
mark (+/- 500 feet). In fact, wildlife studies confirm that most Columbia blacktails prefer to live at elevations of 1,500 feet and lower.

The bucks that live from the 1,500 foot elevation mark, down to
the fringes of valley floors are what I call *foothill blacktails*. Of all the
blacktails I've hunted over the years, these have been the deer I've spent
the most time with. To me, these are the ultimate of all blacktails because they exhibit behaviors that encompass all other blacktails (Cascade, valley floor, coastal, open and high country). Furthermore, they
live in a varied habitat which makes hunting them difficult, from rugged mountains to gentle hills to riparian river bottoms, forests and brush-
choked creek beds.

Foothill blacktails are primarily home-bodies. Generally speaking, they are born, live, and die within a small radius encompassing one to two square miles. While many does appear to have a smaller home range than the bucks, it's the pockets of does which motivate the bucks to cover ground during the rut. This means, late in the season – beginning around the latter part of October – many bucks go on the move, which gives a false appearance of a small-scale migration. In fact, what I've observed happening is a population of mature bucks coming out of hiding and dropping in elevation to find receptive does. They are not migrating; they are on excursions, looking for does and will return to their core areas where they will spend the winter.

These excursion bucks will also spend a good deal of time cruising benches and hillsides at the same elevation, or moving horizontally. I've seen bucks cover nearly two miles in one day of horizontal traveling. During the rut, some blacktail bucks will lay a rub line, much like how a whitetail lays a scrape line. Most of these I've observed have been along horizontal travel routes. Benches and old logging roads are ideal places for bucks to lay rub lines.

One thing I feel that's made foothill bucks more aggressive in recent years is the repercussion felt by a decline in overall deer populations due to Hair Loss Syndrome. Bigger, stronger bucks are the ones who largely survive this disease, therefore there are more of them and with a drop in doe densities, bucks appear to be covering more ground in a competitive effort to find receptive does. As a result, there are some big bucks being taken from the third week in October, all the way up to December in this area.

Foothill blacktails require the most comprehensive hunting approach of all blacktail subgroups for the simple fact they occupy such a wide-range of habitat, not to mention hunting seasons in these areas can start in the summer and may carry through to the middle of December in some units. This means hunters need to know the behavior of these deer during the time they intend to hunt them, and prepare accordingly. From party drives to still-hunting to calling, glassing, using tree stands and more, foothill blacktail hunters may need to pull out all the stops to fill a tag.

**Blacktails living in the foothill region are
primarily resident deer.**

Where foothill bucks leave off, *valley floor blacktails* pick up. Valley floor blacktails are the ones I consider to be year-round home-bodies. Bucks will go into hiding soon after shedding their velvet and may not be seen other than in the rut or during periods of antler growth in the summer months. Often times, big bucks in these areas live and die in a very small core area, without ever being seen by humans. What's interesting here, I believe that many foothill bucks living at lower elevations infiltrate valley blacktail land during the rut. Knowing how and where such bucks move can play a huge part in your success, and much of this comes down to knowing where resident populations of does reside in the valleys.

Valley floor bucks are the ones I consider to be living in lowland drainages adjacent to surrounding hills or mountains. These hills or mountains may be the Cascades, Coast Range, or smaller formations between the two. Valley floor deer lead easy lives compared to other subgroups. They have a year-round food supply in the form of wild vegetation, but they also have access to agricultural lands, man-made grassy meadows, even pastures and lawns.

Because there is so much water in the lower elevations where these deer live, lack of food and moisture are not a concern, nor is snowfall. In other words, these deer lead an easy life. The result can be healthy animals, and if the genetics are good in an area, the bucks can be spectacular.

One of the author's better bucks came from the low elevations of Oregon's Willamette Valley.

One thing I have observed in some valley blacktail populations is a decline in overall body size with an increase in antler size in some of the areas I've hunted over the years. I think the primary reason behind this is people feeding them on private ranches, even in their yards. When this happens, the deer don't get the nutrients required to grow big, either in body or antler. At the same time, I think many of these hand-fed deer become sedentary given their easy lifestyle, and interbreeding also becomes a valid concern.

The reason I even address this issue is because in Washington, Oregon and California, some of the biggest valley floor bucks that are making it into the record books are those that live amid residential areas. The situation is not unlike that of mule deer and whitetails in other parts of the country, and if nothing else, goes to show the wide-range of habitats blacktails can survive in.

Physically speaking, hunting lowland bucks is likely the easiest of all that you'll find in the blacktail world. Though there may be some timbered hills to contend with, for the most part the land is flat. This doesn't mean the hunting is easy. The brush in the lowlands, be it poison oak, willows, or a tangled mess of other vegetation, can make hunting these deer very challenging and frustrating.

I also think some of these lowland bucks are among the smartest of all blacktails for the simple reason they are tuned-in to human activity. This means they know when hunting season starts, and most importantly, know what they have to do to stay alive.

Lowland bucks are likely the easiest deer to pattern in the blacktail world, though I'm still not convinced a blacktail can be patterned like a whitetail or mule deer, at least not on a regular basis. However, with the use of trail cameras it's easy to discover the presence of a buck, and confirm that he's staying in an area.

Hunting lowland bucks is tough due to the simple fact it's nearly impossible to penetrate their thick habitat without spooking them. This is why hunting the edges of meadows early in the morning and at last light is the most common approach. Setting up tree stands and ground blinds are also a good bet in this area. Late in the year, calling can be very effective, especially if you've done your homework and figured out where the does are hanging out.

Moving west through the valleys and into the hills, we encounter another type of deer, what I call the *coastal blacktail*. Coastal blacktails live amid the rugged, dense forests of the Coast Range and are non-migratory, that is, they live in the same area, year-round. They can be found at the summit of the mountain range, all the way down to the

9

beach. For many hunters, they consider these to be the toughest of all blacktails to hunt. In many cases, I would agree.

As if the rugged, brush-choked terrain of the Coast Range isn't enough to overcome, hunters have to deal with a very secretive deer that is used to getting pressured by hunters. The result is one of the toughest hunts in North America, both physically and mentally.

One of the biggest blacktails I ever saw was in the Coast Range. We were hunting Roosevelt elk in the early archery season of September, and deer season was open, too. Glassing the edge of a clearing, I saw a dandy blacktail that would have easily gone over 135-inches. Next to him was a tall, massive 4x4 that I calculated to be about 147-inches. My Roosevelt hunting stopped for the next few days, and despite hunting this buck in every way I could think of, I never saw him again. A 147-inch buck is big for any blacktail, but for a coastal buck, that's a once-in-a-lifetime occurrence. It goes to show how these subgroups of blacktails really are different from one another.

Coastal blacktails can have a small home range, but they will also travel based on their needs and interests. Food is abundant in the Coast Range, as is water, so a big buck's primary focus is to stay alive and

The Coast Range is one of the most challenging habitats in which to hunt trophy blacktails.

breed when the time comes. This means their daily movements can be very minimal and very deliberate, and given the fact they don't have to go far for food and water, they can survive in a very small core area.

For hunters, they have their work cut out for them when it comes to pursuing bucks in the coastal zone. If talking straight archery hunting, I think these are the toughest of all blacktails to kill. This is especially true early in the season, when the ground is so noisy, sneaking up on a buck seems nearly impossible the majority of the time. There's a reason some of California's coastal units are still open to hunting these secretive blacktails with dogs.

But because the use of dogs is not legal in most areas, hunters are dependent upon stealth and smart hunting to secure a coastal deer. Spending time glassing the edges of logged units and clearings, then making a plan of attack is the norm. An increasing number of hunters are also discovering how valuable tree stands can be in this terrain, whether hunting close-quarters with a bow, or long-range with a rifle.

However you choose to hunt coastal blacktails, be ready to put in some serious time and effort. Keep careful track of what you observe in terms of deer behavior, for this information may be highly valuable on future hunts. Finally, be mentally and physically prepared to deal with jungle-like habitat where shots can come at close range.

For a refreshing break from the brush, and a glimpse at the fifth subgroup of blacktails, let's move to the open land and take a look at what I call the *open country blacktails*. Open-country blacktails are deer that live in exactly that, open terrain. Geographically, this habitat begins in west-central Oregon, in the Umpqua River Valley, and runs south all the way through central California. These are non-migratory populations of deer, and can be found in the same area throughout the course of the year.

Typically, the elevation of open country blacktails lies above that of valley floor deer, and below foothill, Cascade and coastal bucks. For blacktail hunters who grew up chasing deer in thick, brushy terrain, there's no greater sense of relief than when hunting bucks in the open. The initial feeling is that of hunting mule deer, and the fact shots can come at long range only drives home the sensation.

Some of Oregon and California's bigger blacktails have come from the open country. Whether they are true blacktails or inland blacktails

11

(by record book standards), the common denominator is that the bucks thrive in open terrain, and their lifestyles differ from other subgroups of blacktails.

Open-country blacktails often feed and bed in or very close to grassland habitats. Because of this, they rely largely on their eyesight for protection. Often, when danger approaches, the deer will simply lay low to the ground, letting the grass be their cover. At the same time, some of these deer will not wander far from brushy fringes, relying on the thick cover for protection.

Their feeding activities may commence in the final minutes of daylight and subside well before daylight, which means early and late in the day hunts are the best times to be afield. Seasonal food sources, though, can keep these deer active during the day. One of my favorite open-country food sources to target is freshly sprouting blackberry bushes during the months of August and September. At this time the deer love eating fresh chutes, and may even bed amid the berry tangles.

Another open-country food source is acorns. When the acorn crop is good, be ready to spend serious time covering the ground in

From west-central Oregon down to California, open country terrain makes up much of the blacktail's habitat

search of bucks. This is where using trail cameras to figure out the caliber and number of bucks in an area can pay off.

Because big, old, open country blacktail bucks can lead a fairly nocturnal lifestyle, be prepared to spend time hunting the land which links covered bedding areas with open country food sources. Often times its on the trails connecting these two areas where bucks are killed, rather than smack in the open. The best time to scout for these bucks is in July and August, when they are in velvet and visibly active during daylight hours.

The racks of bucks in open country also seem to be wider when compared to surrounding blacktail populations, though not as massive overall. This could be due to genetics or a shift in a deer's annual diet. Some folks believe it could possibly be due to bucks spending more time in the open and that their racks have adapted by growing wider, perhaps closer to their true genetic potential. Many blacktail hunters who have not spent time in some of California's prime blacktail land, namely Mendocino or Trinity counties, often dismiss these deer as being crossed with mule deer because their antlers are so big, when in fact this is not the case at all. I think the bucks in these areas grow such big racks because they are able to reach an ideal level of maturity and they have the genetic makeup to do so. They truly show how big blacktail racks are capable of growing. Whatever the case, the rack configuration among open-country bucks is definitely unique, and the older and bigger the buck, the more pronounced the characteristic appears to be.

Behaviorally speaking, these deer could be a bit edgier than other blacktail subgroups. This could be explained by the fact their eyes, nose and ears have to work overtime in the open country, where the bucks seem to be on constant alert rather than being able to relax from time to time in thick cover.

My favorite time of season to hunt open-country bucks is early, when they are still in velvet. Even if the season is not yet open, it's a good time to head afield and look for bucks. This type of scouting will allow you to see what caliber of bucks are in the area, so at least you know what to look for later in the year, when the season opens. If you see them there in velvet, they won't be far come hunting season.

I also like hunting these areas during heavy rain and wind storms, which not only makes for quieter going, but also knocks down valued food sources from the surrounding trees that the deer love, especially mosses, lichens and acorns. The first storm of the season can be the best hunting day, too, so make every effort to be in the field.

Finally, let's take a look at what I like to call the *high country blacktail*, the sixth and final subgroup of the Columbia blacktail deer. If you're a mule deer fan, you'll take a special liking to the high country blacktail. Geographically, these deer are the ones living in the high, rugged back country of northern California, between the Coast Range and Cascade Mountains.

These blacktails are unique in the area they call home, the way they behave and the way they are hunted. High country blacktails are migratory deer, occupying the high elevations in areas such as the Trinity Alps, the Marble Mountains and the Yolla Bolly Wilderness regions, and others like them in the area.

California's Trinity Alps are unique to the world of blacktails, and home to high country deer.

One thing that sets these blacktails apart from others is the fact they migrate to lower elevations quite early. A man I've had the pleasure of hunting with, and who has taken some monster deer from these

14

areas, Parrey Cremeans, knows as much about these deer as anyone I've met, and this is what he has to say.

"When the first full moon in October hits, that's when you'll find the biggest push of migratory deer out of these areas," he begins. "Remember, there are many peaks over 7,000 feet in elevation here, with the highest at about 9,000 feet in the Trinities. I've been on some big bucks at the 8,500 foot level. When up this high in the early season, they depend on lush mountain meadows to sustain them. But because food is so scarce, they'll migrate out of there at the first hint of winter. By mid-October we're seeing lots of deer making their way into their wintering grounds."

Cremeans points out that the deer will browse along their way down to lower elevations, meaning it may take them some time to reach the wintering grounds. I think the key Cremeans hits on here is food dictating the deer's behavior, especially when combined with waning photoperiods.

The high country bucks, even the Cascade bucks of California, don't receive near the moisture content that the Cascade bucks of Washington and Oregon do. Combine the hot summers and falls which quickly dry up food sources, with a rocky, shale-covered environment that doesn't allow much good food to grow in the first place, then throw in the first glimpse of winter, and it's no wonder these deer waste little time moving to areas of better feed at lower elevations.

Cremeans notes that usually by November, snow packs this area above the 4,000 foot level, and all the deer are gone by then. Interestingly, he also points out that wildlife officials have recorded a good number of deer actually swimming across Trinity Lake at night, during their vertical migration.

For hunters, knowing where these early migrating deer are heading is important. These high country bucks lie in California's B Zone, which consists of a great deal of public land, with some private land in the lower elevations. Many of the migrating bucks end up on private land, and that can be tough to access. The good part, B Zone tags can be picked up over-the-counter and loads of public land hunting opportunities abound.

"The primary breeding area for the Trinity Alps deer lays in a triangle, between Highway 299 to the south, Trinity Lake to the west, and

15

Interstate-5 to the east," shares Cremeans. "Some deer will migrate out of the hills and head west, toward the Klamath River area. Some will peel off to the east. We'll pick up lots of sheds in this breeding and wintering area, though, and it's not unusual to see 12 to 15 bucks a day when they have moved into the area during the October hunting season."

But once these deer start moving, they go from the high, open habitat to timber, which means finding them is not easy. Once they start moving they disappear into the brush and feed amid heavy cover as they continue dropping in elevation.

Most of the deer in the B Zone are considered true blacktails. However, this classification does change with the seasons, due to an influx of migratory deer. If nothing else, this shows how unique this population of blacktails really is.

Last but not least, there are the Sitka blacktail deer, *Odocoileus hemionus sitkensis*. These deer range from the northern British Columbia coastline throughout Southeast Alaska's rain forest, up to the Yakutat and Prince William Sound regions. Populations also abound on Afognak and Kodiak islands.

**Kodiak Island is considered by many to offer the best
Sitka blacktail hunting in the world.**

The home range of Sitka blacktails greatly varies depending on terrain. Studies have revealed that a deer's home range can vary from 30 to 1,200 acres. Of course, migratory deer – what I like to call *alpine blacktails* – have a larger home range than nonmigratory deer – what I refer to as *forest blacktails*. Migratory deer have been recorded traveling up to five miles while resident deer have shown to move a mere half-mile during the course of the year.

As the winter snow pack begins to melt, migratory Sitka blacktails begin moving to higher elevations in the alpine and subalpine habitats, while resident deer remain at lower elevations amid the forest. With the first heavy frost, deer in the higher alpine and subalpine regions begin to descend to the lower elevations where food is available and protection from the elements exists.

In forested regions throughout the rest of the winter and early spring, deer are generally restricted to uneven-aged, old-growth forest below 1,500 feet in elevation. This zone provides optimal winter habitat because the high, broken canopy intercepts much snow yet still allows enough light in for the growth of food sources. Deer in more open habitats at this time, like on parts of Kodiak and Afognak Island, will spend time in lower elevations among alder thickets and tall grass.

During the late fall and winter hunting season, changing snow depth is what most impacts the distribution of Sitka deer at various elevations. When the snow accumulation is extreme, many deer congregate in heavily timbered areas, even along beaches. Spring is a very critical time for Sitka blacktails, for if late snows are deep and persistent, many deer die of starvation. This is why it's important to phone ahead to regional Alaska Department of Fish and Game offices prior to going on a hunt, to see how the previous winter's survival rates fared.

Hunting Sitka blacktails is addicting, if nothing else, for the sheer number of animals you'll likely see. It's not uncommon to see 50 deer a day. I've spent several days afield where we've seen over 100 deer in a single day. When conditions are ideal and herd numbers healthy, this can be some of the most exciting blacktail hunting you'll ever experience.

Hunts can be as easy as cruising the beaches or driving logging roads, finding a buck and stalking to within shooting range. Then again, if pursuing alpine bucks, the hunting can be as physically demanding as any deer hunt you've encountered. These bucks often respond well to calls and decoys during the rut, which makes them even more thrilling to chase.

As this book progresses you'll continue reading about detailed references to overall blacktail behavior and specific hunting approaches that will relate to the six Columbia blacktail and two Sitka blacktail subgroups that have been highlighted here. Keep in mind that the subgroups I just covered are not necessarily unique, at least not by genetic standards. However, due to the wide range of habitats blacktail deer occupy, and the range of behaviors they exhibit based on the terrain in which they live, I feel it's vital to get to know each of these deer in order to gain a more thorough understanding of their behavior, thus, how to hunt them.

Life-Cycle

Detailed looks at the biology and behavior of blacktail deer will follow in each subsequent chapter, but here, let's take a general look at some factors and characteristics which delineate these animals. Knowing such information is crucial to gaining a more complete comprehension for how these deer live.

Blacktail deer belong to the *Order Artiodactyla*, which is characterized by a four-chamber stomach, toes that form hooves and molars. This classification points out the obvious fact these deer are herbivores and require time to lay down, regurgitate their food and chew it again.

For years it was accepted that the Columbia blacktail deer was a subspecies of the mule deer. Now, up-to-date DNA tests have revealed mule deer are, in fact, descendants of blacktails and whitetails having crossed. More specifically, the research has concluded that it was the actual mating of whitetail does and blacktail bucks that produced the mule deer.

It's now thought that hundreds-of-thousands of years ago the whitetail expanded its range from the eastern United States, south into and across Mexico, then back up the West Coast. Here, it's believed the deer evolved into the blacktail deer. This is interesting in the fact that it not only explains why some blacktail racks may look so much like whitetails, but also why their behaviors are so similar.

Over the next several thousands of years, the blacktail evolved and its range spread eastward, where it overlapped with the westward expanding whitetail. Blacktails were once believed to have ranged as far east as Wyoming. In the places where the two deer overlapped, whitetail bucks are believed to have been displaced by more aggressive blacktail bucks, and crossbreeding of the two species took place. The result of this crossing is the mule deer.

Blacktail deer derive their name from the coloration on the outside of the tail, which is black from the base of the tail to its tip. The underside is white.

Blacktail bucks will average 120-180 pounds on the hoof. Depending on what geographic setting the bucks come from, their weight range can vary. Over the decades, the biggest blacktails my family has taken have come from the foothill region. We've taken several bucks here that weighed between 180 and 210 pounds with the biggest tipping the scale to 216, another to 211 pounds.

Though I've taken record book bucks from the valley floor, Cascades and open-country, none of these bucks have weighed more than 175 pounds. A big 6x6 I arrowed one season from the valley floor barely went 130 pounds, yet his rack carried more than 130-inches.

Sitka blacktails, though smaller in body and antler size, still grow bigger than what many people think. While Sitka bucks average about 120

MARK GLASSMAKER PHOTO

Sitka blacktails could well be the most striking of all North America's deer.

19

pounds, reports of deer weighing over 200 pounds have been confirmed. One year while hunting Kodiak Island, we took a buck that weighed 204 pounds. A buddy who has hunted Kodiak for over three decades has taken a surprising number of bucks in the 190-210-pound class.

Generally, the lifespan of both the Columbia and Sitka blacktail is about 10 years, with some exceptions living beyond 12 years. Once bucks have reached six or seven years of age, they're considered to be in prime trophy condition, meaning their rack formations are optimal. At the age of eight, a buck's antlers usually begin to decline in quality. Overall, bucks don't live as long as does due to the stresses and reduced body conditions incurred during the rut. In Oregon, ODF&W studies show that few bucks live beyond nine years of age, while many does live up to 15 years.

Columbia blacktail bucks start dropping their antlers in January, and are typically done with the process by the end of February. Sitka blacktails can shed their antlers as early as mid-December, and are usually done by mid-January. Antler shedding is the result of a shift in hormonal production after the rut and during the height of winter.

July and August are some of the best times to scout for trophies like this big buck in velvet.

Antler growth commences in early spring, and by mid-June hunters can head afield scouting for bucks. Though the antlers still have a couple months of growing time left, bucks can be sized-up for a fairly accurate projection of how big they will eventually be.

Late June, all of July and early August are some of the best times to scout and physically see big bucks. At this time, their antlers are still in velvet and these blood-rich tissues are very sensitive. To protect themselves against the anguish, bucks often spend all day in open areas, so as not to risk hitting their racks against limbs and brush, which can be painful and cause malformations in their headgear. Look in shaded areas for bucks bedding during hot, midday hours.

Beginning around the middle of August and sometimes as late as early September, the bucks will start rubbing the drying velvet off their antlers. The shedding of velvet, once it starts, is usually finished within a few days for all the bucks in a given area. As soon as this happens, many of the big bucks go into hiding, and become more active at night.

September through October is a time of pre-rut for blacktail bucks. This is when they focus on accumulating food for the upcoming rut and winter months, and take note of what does are in the area. They'll also size-up bucks in the region, which may later be competition come the rut. Some sparring takes place at this time, but it's not to be confused with a fight for dominance which happens during the rut. Often times people see bucks sparring in late September and early October and reason that the rut is starting early, when this is not actually the case.

Personally, I believe the blacktail rut is one of the least understood phenomenons in the deer hunting world. I will detail my thoughts on this topic more in chapters 4 and 5, but for now suffice it to say that typically, the rut can run from mid-October through December.

When a doe comes into heat, or is receptive to breed, she has a 24-hour fertile period. During this first estrus cycle is when most of the does get bred. If they miss being bred in the first estrus cycle, they'll come into heat again, 28 days later. Interestingly, during the second estrus period, the pH of the doe's hormones changes, which results in a greater likelihood of bucks being born. This is nature's way of population control, for if a doe is missed being bred in her first cycle, it could be due to the fact not enough bucks were around.

Blacktail bucks are polygamous, or have more than one mate. Prior to the peak of the rut, bucks will know what does are in their territory. Once the rut approaches, bucks will cruise from doe herd to doe herd searching for females that have come into heat. This is sensed by the odor in her urine, which the buck can not only smell on the ground, but can detect through molecules in the air as well.

The gestation period of a blacktail doe is about 200 days. This means a doe that gives birth on June 1 would have been bred about November 7th. When a doe drops her fawn, or fawns, depends on when she is bred.

Knowing precisely when blacktail fawns are born tells you a lot about the deer in an area, including when the rut took place.

I've been spring bear hunting in Southeast Alaska, where Sitka blacktail populations are thick, and saw one or two fawns a day. Then, on the next day, June 2nd to be exact, we saw over 20 fawns. The day after that we counted over 30 fawns. This proves that the breeding of all these does took place within a couple days of one another, and also shows that buck densities are high in this area given the fact nearly every doe had fawns. Knowing this information, if I were to return

22

and hunt that area for deer in the fall, I'd be sure and be there from November 4-12, to ensure I hit the peak rutting period based on last year's activities. It would also be good hunting from the middle of November through the first week in December, when bucks are searching for does they missed breeding in the first cycle.

When nutritious food is plentiful, does will usually give birth to their first fawn at two years of age. Twins are common after that, and they can continue producing fawns up to about 12 years of age, sometimes longer. For Sitka blacktails, May and June, depending on where you hunt blacktails, is a good time to be afield to see for yourself when the fawns are being dropped. These dates, in turn, provide direct correlation to when the actual breeding took place. As a general rule, the rut will take place about the same time the following year. This is good information for hunters to know, especially if fawns are being seen in late April or early May, which indicates rutting activity took place early the previous fall.

Starvation during the winter months is the primary cause of blacktail fatalities. For some populations of Sitka blacktails, heavy winter and early spring snows can claim a majority of the entire population. This has happened on places like Kodiak and Afognak islands, repeatedly. Infestation by parasites is the second leading cause of death. With the onset of Deer Hair Loss Syndrome, some populations of Columbia blacktails have been decimated.

Cougars are a major predator of blacktail deer. Ed Miller took this big tom from the Cascade Range.

23

The leading predators of blacktail deer are coyotes, bobcats, cougar, domestic dogs and bears. Deer are very susceptible to predation during fawning and also during harsh winters. While coyotes are the number one predator of Columbia blacktail fawns, bobcats also claim a high number in the spring and summer months. Blacktail hunters looking to help maintain healthy herds will want to spend serious time hunting and even trapping predators in the areas they hunt. Organized events like the one developed by the Mendocino County Blacktail Association – a coyote hunting competition held in the summer – can make a difference in keeping predator numbers in check, thus aide in overall blacktail population enhancement.

Diet

When it comes to food, blacktails have an incredibly diverse diet. Deer in coastal habitats have been recorded eating up to 62 different kinds of plants, with leaves making up nearly 60% of the diet. Depending on the time of year, geographic setting and conditions, blacktails will feed on several varieties of grass and woody plants, too.

In the spring blacktails eat lush, tender grasses and other newly sprouting forms of vegetation and forbs. Scout for big bucks feeding on south-facing slopes this time of year as this is where the most food growth occurs. The spring is an important time for bucks to find protein-rich (nitrogen) food in order to optimize antler growth. For adult deer to attain optimal health and growth, their diet must consist of approximately 14% crude protein, or about 9% digestible protein.

In the early summer months, look for blacktail bucks to continue feeding on southern slopes, but moving more toward the west-facing slopes as daylight hours lengthen. As the summer progresses and the south and west slopes dry up, deer will still search for green grass and forbs amid shaded and moist areas. Their diet will also include wild clover and mushrooms this time of year. One thing I've observed in the areas I hunt is that when other food sources are available, mushrooms can go overlooked. I think sometimes hunters place too much emphasis on mushrooms being a primary food source of deer, as when they find standing groups of fungi that haven't been devoured, dismiss it to there being no deer in the area. This is a mistake, since deer don't always feed on fungi.

Also in the summer, deer continue feeding on fresh sprouting leaves of deciduous trees and bushes. They will also feast on sword ferns, kelp and grass in beach areas, and they love the new shoots of trailing blackberries. In fact, trailing blackberries are found to be the most preferred, most nutritious food of the blacktail deer where it occurs in their home range. They also like the leaves of other forms of berry plants, and when they start to ripen, the berries themselves. Because weeds grow well in summer, these also become a much utilized food source. There are numerous forms of noxious weeds deer will feed on in the summer, from dandelions to Queen Ann's Lace to thistles. As acorns begin to drop in late summer, these are also highly prized by blacktails.

In late summer and early fall, blacktails will eat many forms of berries. Blackberries, red huckleberries, thimbleberries, snow berries, cranberries, Oregon grape, wild strawberries, crow berries, salmon berries and salal berries are some of the fruits they'll seek out. In lowland habitat areas, deer will also go out of their way to access fruit orchards, namely apple and pear. Some of the best blacktail haunts are those near old growth apple orchards planted by homesteaders in the region.

Other forms of food blacktails like that have been introduced by humans include a wide range of agricultural crops (grains, grasses, vegetables and flowers), grape vineyards, Christmas tree farms, nurseries and reforested areas. Because these foods are nurtured for human use, they provide a reliable food source many deer have become dependent upon, even to the point where they prefer them over natural forms of vegetation.

As fall gives way to winter, deer will return to feeding on grasses that have greened-up, along with oak leaves and more, depending on the area they live in. When the herbaceous food sources dwindle, blacktails start feeding more on woody tissues. They like eating huckleberry twigs, vine maple, sword fern and evergreen salal this time of year, too. One of their favorites is ceanothus, or buckbrush. This is a critical time for deer, for what they eat in the winter carries very little nutrient value. Branches, boughs of conifers, twigs, mosses, mistletoe and lichens will be consumed, along with tree bark when food becomes scarce. All the deer are hoping to do at this point is survive, not necessarily improve their health.

By the end of winter and into early spring, many of the deer droppings you find will be runny and often clumped together. This is a sign that they are not receiving the nutrients needed to maintain a healthy body. But shortly after spring growth sprouts, the deer's digestive system starts maximizing its food intake and their bodies capitalize on protein-packed foods which are now available. As spring turns the corner, the deer that made it through winter start recovering and building healthy bodies once again.

One of the main creators of ideal blacktail food, and habitat, is fire. Fire, be it man made or natural, creates some of the absolute best feeding conditions a blacktail deer could ask for. In recent years the lack of logging, and access to private logging areas, has likely had the most negative impact on trophy blacktail deer hunting.

Fire clears many forms of non-protein rich vegetation deer don't benefit from, and creates ideal conditions for new growth to thrive in. It is the new growth, especially in the form of herbaceous browse and to some degree, grasses, that most benefits blacktails.

With rain comes green grass, one of the many food sources of blacktails.

Where fires have swept through blacktail areas, the first rains of fall often bring fresh sprouting grass. Deer love this new food source. For the next three to five years, sometimes more in higher elevations, new foods will continue to sprout, and hunters should make a conscious effort to hunt these places. Elk and mule deer hunters capitalize on burns to find big animals, and so should blacktail hunters.

Even the controlled burns of logging operations can create enough prime forage that deer will actively seek out such areas. In fact, logged units can be exceptional deer habitats. The act of logging opens up the forest canopy and allows the new growth of valued foods to take place along the timbered fringes. These are some of the best habitats and food sources a blacktail hunter could ask for.

Even within a year after being logged, the actual units themselves will start attracting deer. As the unit matures and more varieties of food continue to grow, still more deer will come. When units reach about five years of age, they are considered prime for trophy blacktail hunters. At this age the unit provides a wide range of food types and enough cover that big bucks feel comfortable taking up residency in and around them.

However, recent logging practices in some areas have changed to the point of altering deer habitats. For example, today many logging companies poison out logged units rather than burning them, or burn them then poison them. Their purpose is to cut down on weeds, grasses and other vegetation that compete with planted conifers. The outcome is degradation of what should be prime blacktail habitat, and the final result is the deer are forced to move out of the area.

The exception to changing logging practices is on Prince of Wales Islands, and other islands in Southeast Alaska, where the forest is so fertile and regrowth is so fast, prime food flourishes. The only thing that's changed here in recent years is there is far less logging than there used to be.

Due to the geographic region the Sitka blacktail calls home, their diet obviously differs a bit when compared to their Columbian cousins. During the summer months, Sitka blacktails primarily feed on the green leaves of shrubs and other herbaceous vegetation. In late summer and early fall, they like the woody brows and even the fruit of huckleberries, blueberries and salmon berries.

In the winter months, Sitka blacktails are generally restricted to feeding on evergreen forbs and woody browse. Willow thickets and patches of devil's club are favorites. The evergreen forbs of trailing bramble and bunchberry can be key food sources in getting deer through

winter when deep snow is not a concern. During periods of deep snow, woody browse such as yellow cedar, hemlock, willows, blueberries and arboreal lichens are consumed.

As with Columbia blacktails, Sitka blacktails cannot meet their bodily needs solely through the eating woody browse. A diet of woody tissues depletes the deer's body of valued energy reserves when restricted to such forage. This is where it gets dangerous for these deer, for should late, deep snows fall, the deer become susceptible to starvation.

Sitka blacktails have a wide-range of vegetation which they rely on.

When planning a hunting trip for trophy blacktails, do the research to learn what the past few winters have been like in the area, and how it has impacted deer numbers. See if fires or logging may offer a bonus food source to capitalize on. The more thoroughly you cover details, the better the chance of seeing your name in the record book.

Hair Loss Syndrome

While harsh winters can claim the lives of Columbia blacktail deer, so too can disease. There are some diseases known to infect and kill blacktails, but for the most part these diseases are short-lived in the areas they sweep through, or eventually the deer build up immunity to them. However, there is one syndrome that has impacted blacktail populations like no other, and it's not going away.

It's called Deer Hair Loss Syndrome (DHLS) and is something blacktail hunters need to know about. Why? Because not only is it decimating blacktail populations in historically rich habitats, but I think it's changing the dynamics of buck behavior in elevations below 1,500 feet, where the disease is present in Oregon, and below 2,500 feet, where the disease is present in Washington. Knowing the basic details of this syndrome can help you kill more mature bucks, which, by the way, are the least impacted by DHLS.

Initially recognized in 1992 and officially confirmed a few years later in the Puget Sound area of Washington, DHLS made its way into western Oregon in 1996. Since then it has spread throughout much of western Washington and Oregon and has made its way into northern California. DHLS is referred to as a syndrome, not a disease, because the cause and transmission means are not totally understood. Where it will stop, no one knows.

The DHLS condition is caused by a louse that's smaller than a flea. Thought to have made it's way into Washington from Asia or Africa, this louse, called *Damalinia Cervicola*, actually chews on a deer's skin to the point it causes the deer to excessively itch, rub and groom itself, an act called pruritus, to the point hair loss occurs. Deer can die from the stress of this condition, as well as by exposure caused by the uncontrolled hair loss.

Because the stress of DHLS can so intensely impact a deer's life, there is often a breakdown in their body's defense system, meaning they become susceptible to infestation by parasites as well as more vulnerable to hypothermia and other disease. These factors, then, can kill deer.

How DHLS is transmitted is not 100% certain, but researchers believe it can be passed from deer to deer by direct contact, through water, air (sneezing), from the ground (bed and trail sharing), and through parasite sharing. At this time there are no documented instances of humans, pets or livestock becoming sick from contacting deer carrying symptoms of DHLS. There are also no known health risks to humans consuming the meat of infected deer, just make sure it's cooked properly, like all game meat.

Not all blacktails acquire DHLS. Deer that are initially in poor health, usually from a lack of nutrients in their diet or have faced a harsh winter are the ones hit the hardest. This can explain why some deer in a herd may have DHLS and others may not. Fawns are the most susceptible to the contraction of DHLS due to their week immune system – which can lead to very poor fawn survival in some areas – followed by adult females. In some areas of study in Oregon, more than 80% of fawns and 40% of does were found to be affected by DHLS. In Oregon's Willamette Valley, home to some of the best black-tail hunting, surveys have revealed up to 80% of newborn fawns to be affected by DHLS and carry a 60% mortality rate which equates to a total loss of nearly 50% of all fawns. Bucks, especially older bucks, are least effected by the syndrome and it's potentially fatal side effects.

If a deer does survive its first winter of DHLS, it's not known if its chance of survival increases the following winter should it become infested again. Studies conducted in Oregon have revealed that an affected animal can carry up to 30 times the number of lice in winter than it does in summer. It's also been learned that the louse can live up to a week on the ground (like in a deer's bed), depending on the temperature, which means it's easy for the organism to jump hosts.

The physical characteristics deer display that have been infected with DHLS varies with the changing seasons. In mid-winter to mid-spring, hair loss is evident and the hair in the midsection of the body, flanks, rump and along the neck is quite yellow, even white. Infected deer will display excessive itching, lethargy, look emaciated and have diarrhea. From late spring to early fall, the deer that survive will regrow their hair and regain weight. During the summer months, the louse can be nonexistent on deer. As fall progresses and winter fur grows, the louse will infest the deer once again and a darkening coat appears. Patches of hair will also start to fall out, especially in the midsection of the deer.

My first up-close encounter with an infected deer was in December of 2002. The yearling came up to our covered porch and nestled against the house for warmth. There was snow on the ground, it was windy and cold and the deer sought protection from the elements. The little deer was very skinny; its sides were white in color. It was missing close to 75% of its winter coat, and what was left of its pelage appeared abnormally scruffy. Two days later another infected yearling did the same thing at the neighbor's house. Within three days, both deer were dead.

**Deer Hair Loss Syndrome has had a major
impact on some blacktail populations.**

Since then I've observed hundreds of infected deer on a year-round
basis, and those hardest hit are definitely the younger populations and
the does, especially when having to face hard winters. I've also seen
several Columbia whitetails in west-central Oregon infected by DHLS.
The syndrome is scary, and as scientists continue to learn more about
it, they will do their best to inform the public. For a more detailed look
at the science behind this syndrome and what's being learned about it,
contact state wildlife authorities or visit their websites for updates.

At the time of this writing there are no known treatments for DHLS.
Trying to contain it is an almost impossible task, or so it seems. Some
areas of Oregon have experienced more than a 50% reduction in blacktail numbers, with the coastal mountains being among the hardest hit.
That's what's so scary about this disease; it seems to have no boundaries other than cold temperatures.

DHLS is now confirmed in western Washington from the coastal
islands, inland to the western slopes of the Cascade Mountains up to
about 2,500 feet in elevation, and from British Columbia in the north

to the state's southern boundaries along the Columbia River. In Oregon, it's made its way through the western half of the state, from the coast to approximately 1,500 feet in elevation along portions of the western Cascades, and down to the California border. How DHLS will progress in California is unknown. Let's hope it stops.

As time passes, look for DHLS to continue affecting isolated blacktail populations which have not yet been infected. It seems the only hope for this unfortunate problem to go away is for the deer to eventually develop immunity to it. Let's pray they do it quickly, as hunter numbers have already dropped considerably in the blacktail woods of Oregon and Washington, and some seasons have been altered to account for high mortality rates due to DHLS.

So what does this mean for trophy blacktail hunters? It comes down to population dynamics. Interestingly, big bucks continue to be taken in specific areas which have been affected by DHLS. In fact, there has been a large number of big blacktail bucks taken in some infected areas near where I spend most of my time hunting, than I can ever remember. If you stop and think about why, it makes sense.

My theory is not based on any scientific numbers, just observations of deer behavior while personally spending many days a year in the field studying them. As stated earlier, the area in which my family has done most of our blacktail hunting since the mid-1900s is in the foothill region of west-central Oregon's Cascade Mountains. We also spend a good deal of time chasing valley floor bucks as well as some open-country deer in the same general area. In all of these areas, DHLS is prevalent, in fact, some of the worst infestations can be found in some of the pockets we hunt.

There's no question overall deer numbers have declined where we hunt. With fawn and doe survival rates markedly down, why are we still killing big bucks there? Why, if so many fawns are dying, do there continue to be big bucks in the area? When DHLS first made its way into these areas, I wondered how long it would be until it reached the point no big bucks were around. It hasn't happened in the areas I hunt. Not yet, anyway.

In the habitats we hunt, I believe there are still good numbers of healthy bucks for two reasons. First, it's been confirmed that the bucks are more likely to survive a bout with DHLS than does and fawns, which means proportionately the buck to doe ratio is higher. Second - keeping in mind that blacktails are not herd animals like mule deer, rather live in little populations here and there – one pocket of deer may be infected with DHLS, yet another pocket a short distance away may not be infected.

This means that as infected populations of does die, other healthy deer begin to take their place. Though these new does are few in number and may not adopt the exact habitat to call home as the deer before them did, they are still in the same general area and they are healthy. Come rutting time, the big bucks will find them.

Hang with me; this is where it gets interesting. Amid some of these renewed deer populations will be bucks, including young bucks that may have survived DHLS exposure. Now, since bigger bucks have survived any bout they may have had with DHLS, they will compete with these smaller bucks for breeding rights. These big bucks don't necessarily live in the core area where the does and younger bucks do.

I believe the bucks living in the foothill habitats are possibly covering more ground now during the rut than they did eight years prior. I think this to be so because during my spring and summer scouting trips, I'm not seeing the number of bucks I used to, nor any sign of them. Furthermore, I'm not finding the number of antler sheds I did in the past. This means the density of resident bucks in the area has declined. Whether they've relocated to be closer to more does or have simply retreated into deeper cover, perhaps at higher elevations where they are not affected by DHLS, I cannot say.

Even in areas with DHLS, there are some big bucks to be had.

33

But what I have observed are more competitive mature bucks in recent years, and I think they are getting active earlier than what they used to. Why are they getting active earlier? I speculate that many of the doe populations have become so spread out, with the individual group size being smaller, that the bucks try and cover more ground than they formerly had to in order to breed the maximum number of does.

More support for my theory is substantiated in my many observations of does in the areas we hunt dropping fawns around the 4th of July, even later. This means these does were not bred in the first estrus cycle, either because the bucks weren't there, they were off seeking other does, or simply because there weren't any bucks present at the lower elevations to breed the existing does.

Still another valuable clue lies in the increasing number of big bucks I've rattled in and killed during the first week in December, while archery hunting. In the areas I hunt, the bucks are ruttier than they ever were at this time; at least that appears to be the case. It could simply be that few bucks are in the area, and the ones that do move in to breed does are so occupied in covering ground to make sure they don't miss a doe slipping into heat, that they actually miss breeding quite a few estrous does that become receptive when a buck is gone.

Another event I've noticed in some of the areas we hunt suffering big population declines due to DHLS is that the bucks are more aggressive earlier than in previous years. I think this speaks more of the buck's hormonal condition than the does, as the does will come into estrous at specific times of the year, usually every year. Bucks, however, are like the males of many mammalian species in that they are ready to play despite the receptiveness of the does. This is one of nature's ways of ensuring the fittest of the bucks earn the breeding rights to the does.

So, why might these deer be rutting earlier in these areas? It has to do with competition, the fight for dominance and the will to pass on genes. The earlier a buck establishes his dominance and displaces insubordinate bucks, the greater his chances of being the breeding buck. This phenomenon has occurred is in the lower elevations and coastal habitats I hunt, where deer populations are not impacted by a potential influx of migratory bucks. In other words, the bucks in the area are there year-round, and they know what does and other bucks are there, too. To get a jump on the breeding hierarchy, the bucks seem to be fighting earlier and chasing does earlier, though the does may not yet be receptive. On several occasions I've watched mature 4x4 bucks chasing does on October 15th, 16th and 17th. This is very early for the areas I was hunting, where the rut historically didn't occur until about mid-November. In these same areas I've used distressed fawn calls and rattling to pull in bucks as early as October 16th.

My overall conclusion when hunting areas affected by DHLS is to be aggressive, start early and go late. If you're a rifle hunter, mid-October isn't too early to start calling and rattling blacktails. If you're an archery hunter or have a special draw gun or muzzleloader permit, keep calling and rattling all the way to the middle of December.

As doe numbers continue to decline in some areas, do your homework in the off season by learning what the doe populations are. Even if there are a few scattered here and there, the bucks will find them come breeding season. And with the competition growing more for these breeding rights, the bucks are seemingly becoming more aggressive early, prior to the peak of the rut, and carrying it out longer to make certain they hit does that were missed during their first estrous cycle.

Yes, overall, DHLS is not a good thing; not for the deer, not for hunters. But I'm not going to stop hunting blacktails because of it. I'm going to get out there, learn what's happening with the population dynamics in the areas I hunt, and then be aggressive in my hunting approach. If the bucks have to cover more ground to find does, so will I in an effort to find them. If the does have been wiped out of an area, then I'll move to new areas and keep searching until I find them. These approaches have been working for me since DHLS has hit our prime hunting grounds, so I'm going to keep doing what works to keep filling tags. I encourage fellow hunters to do the same.

Record Book Classifications

Attaining a blacktail buck that qualifies for the record book is the dream of many hunters. The question is, in which record book do you want it to be represented? Some books that have been penned on blacktails detail the various record books, their qualification standards and how to score a deer. Given it's already been done, and the fact these pieces of information can easily be gathered from internet websites and various hunting organizations, I'm not going to take the space to go over it here.

There are several record books out there, from Boone & Crockett, to Pope & Young, Safari Club International, Longhunter Muzzleloader and more, including various regional and state record books. Some have the same qualification standards, some are different. Some recognize bucks taken in velvet, those with differing ranges and non-typicals, some don't.

I think the most valuable pieces of information to be gained from each of these record books is not the actual score of the racks, but where they came from. Study these books to see in which counties or locations the trophy bucks were taken. This information, above all else, will confirm that premium genetics are present in those areas, whereby solidifying the fact that these are the places trophy hunters will want to focus on.

It's interesting to look at where some of the record book entry bucks were taken back in the mid-1900s, and where bucks taken from more recent years are coming from. In California you'll notice Mendocino and Trinity counties appearing with regularity. In Oregon, Jackson, Linn, Lane and Clackamas counties dominate the scene, with a host of others being represented. In Washington, Lewis County still ranks number one, with Pierce and King counties also appearing with regularity.

Keep in mind that not everyone who kills record book bucks chooses to enter them. My family, for instance, has taken numerous bucks that would meet the minimum qualifications to appear in several record books (gun, bow and muzzleloader), yet have never done so. Maybe I should, it's just something I've never taken the time to do. I certainly have nothing against it.

At the same time, when looking at record books, some titles may carry heavy representation from one area over another. Take the Safari Club International Record Book, for instance, where a large majority of the bucks entered are from California. This simply means that more hunters belonging to this organization, and who choose to enter their blacktail deer scores, are doing most of their hunting in California. It doesn't necessarily mean fewer big bucks are being taken in Oregon, Washington and British Columbia, rather that there aren't as many entered from these areas.

For Sitka blacktails, Kodiak Island and Prince of Wales Island dominate representation in the record books, with a few coming from British Columbia and other pockets of southeast Alaska. Interestingly, Sitka blacktails are not indigenous to Kodiak Island, yet the habitat is prime for turning out monster bucks. Blacktails made it to Kodiak Island when nine deer were transplanted there in 1934, from the Petersburg area. Today the deer are thriving and have even expanded their range to other islands; they are strong swimmers. The downfall on Kodiak Island is harsh winters and springs, which can decimate deer populations on the island to the point it takes years to recover. This happened during the winter of 1998-1999.

Record books are a valuable tool for hunters to learn from. Not only do they offer information on how to judge and score deer, but they also reveal where the big bucks are coming from. Being a member of the various organizations which publish these books is also a good way to gain further insight and updated information as to what's happening with North America's big game species, including the blacktail deer.

Trophy Judging Racks

For a hunter, the blacktail deer is not an easy big game animal to trophy judge. This is because mature deer live in such thick habitat and the fact that when spooked, only fleeting glimpses may be caught.

Often times, a buck's rack has to be judged in a split-second. This is especially true for still-hunters carrying a rifle or muzzleloader. The key in efficiently judging a trophy animal lies in the skill of being able to locate a buck and observe him, and making certain he's unaware of your presence while you carry out some quick calculations. There's no substitute for smart, patient hunting in this situation.

When a buck is located, the longer you can look at him the more accurately you'll be able to judge his rack. Some important numbers to remember when gauging a buck's rack are as follows. Mind you, these are averages that I've calculated on bucks I've measured over the years, and are just that, averages.

Generally speaking, the average length of a blacktail's ears is about

6-1/4 inches from tip to base. The average width across the middle of the ear is 3-1/2 inches. Knowing the different ear measurements of a deer will help in estimating not only the width of the rack, but more importantly the depth of the forks. If looking for a buck that will qualify for the record books, check each fork closely to make sure the front and back splits closely match one another on each side of the rack. The more symmetry a rack has, the fewer deductions it will carry.

When it comes to judging the mass of a deer's antlers, the eyeball is a valuable tool. The distance from the back of they eyeball to the front edge of the tear duct (diameter) is about 1-1/4 inches, on average. The most important measurement however is the circumference of the eyeball, which is about 3-1/2 inches. A mature blacktail buck will carry about 3-1/2 to 4 inch bases, while exceptional bucks will sport 4-1/2 to 6 inches of mass at the base. A buck with more than 5 inches of mass is outstanding.

The distance from the tip of the nose to the inside corner of the eye is 7 inches. This is a good measurement to know when the buck gives you a profile angle to look at. When looking side-on at a buck, compare the distance from nose tip to the corner of the eye with the height of each fork. This is also a good time to evaluate the main beam length.

Perhaps the measurement most hunters go by is ear to ear spread which is the distance from one tip of the ear to the other. When a buck is relaxed, and his ears are turned out away from the head in a natural, relaxed position, the tip-to-tip ear span can range from 16 to 19 inches. The rule of thumb many hunters go by is 17 inches from ear tip to ear tip. Again, this can vary depending on the genetic makeup of the animals being hunted and the region you're hunting in. I've measured earspans on blacktails over 20 inches and several barely over 16 inches.

Keep in mind these numbers will vary from one deer population to another. One of the biggest bucks I killed had the smallest ears and eyes of any I've seen. Likewise, coastal bucks tend to have smaller measurements than hill country deer, and this is especially true for Sitka blacktails.

With these numbers, you can use a buck's facial features to judge – fairly accurately – his antler size. If the rack spans outside the ears, you're likely looking at a good buck. But more important than antler span, if you're looking to score on a record book buck, is the depth of the forks. This is where knowing the length and width of the ear comes in handy.

If the depth of the forks approaches the overall length of the ear, you're looking at a dandy buck. If all four forks – front and back, left and right side – carry good depth, it's a buck you want to shoot. There are many bucks in various record books that carry spreads less than 20 inches, but score well due to their symmetrically deep forks and good mass. This is where you earn a great deal of points. Spread isn't everything.

Trophy judging a blacktail deer is tough, as rarely do hunters get to observe them in the open for any length of time.

For a quick rundown on field judging Sitka blacktail racks, here are some key numbers to know. The average ear to ear spread is about 14 inches. The average length of the ear is 5 inches, while the average width is about 2-1/2 inches. The distance from the tear duct to the tip of the nose is about 6 inches. The eyeball diameter and circumference is similar to that of a Columbia blacktail, about 1-1/4 and 3-1/2 inches, respectively. Due to the smaller features of a Sitka deer, especially the ear to ear spread and the eye to nose distance, many people overestimate the size of the rack they are looking at. Be careful not to make the same mistake if a record book buck is what you have your sights set on.

Before heading into the field, take the time to memorize these figures. By knowing the size of a buck's facial anatomy – eyes, ears, and various measurements – you can then use them as a template to closely assess how big its rack is. This can be a humbling experience, and is the best teaching tool that I've found when it comes to judging racks on the hoof. Often times, the tendency is to overestimate how big a rack is, resulting in ground shrinkage once you approach the animal. Learn the numbers listed above, compare them to a buck's rack, and you'll be amazed at how quickly you can become a good judge of live deer.

Because it's so difficult to judge a live, mature blacktail buck in the wild, the best teaching tool I've found to help me learn these skills is going to a sport show or hunting convention where mounted bucks are on display. Even better, hit a show where organizations are carrying out antler competitions.

At such events, stand back and look at racks, then crunch the numbers in your head, then look to see what the animals scored. Another valuable aide can be watching these official measurers at work. By watching how they lay a tape to a rack – be it a shoulder mount, skull and rack, even sheds – and seeing what numbers they really end up with, you'll gain valued input that will no doubt help you hone your field-judging skills.

The Mental Game

The mentality of a successful trophy blacktail deer hunter is different from that of the casual, recreational hunter. The attitude consists of a desire and expectation to succeed on all levels, and their thoughts are consumed, year-round, by blacktails. When you arrive at this stage, you're a blacktail addict, and come hunting season, no other big game animal dominates the mind like these deer can.

One of my most memorable blacktail seasons was when both my wife and I hunted together, trying to get her a trophy buck. We'd hunted 15 straight days, and on the afternoon of the 16th day, we nearly got her the dream buck she'd been wanting.

It was late October, pouring down rain, and we went to a place where we'd seen big bucks before, but never taken any monsters. Despite the heavy rain, the timing was right to try rattling. With a synthetic rattle bag – I like these tools when I want to project a loud "fight" beyond what natural antlers are capable of doing – we set up on the edge of a clearing.

A dense creek bottom was below us amid a mix of conifer and deciduous trees. A thicket of tall, green scotch broom grew on the eastern border of the timber line. Trails were thick in this area, and many led to the edge of the meadow in which we sat.

Our thinking was the rut would be kicking-in any day, and that we might be able to pull a big buck out of the woods via rattling. We were right. Less than five minutes into the rattling sequence, a white throat patch caught our eye on the edge of the timber. A jet-black pate topped by a heavy set of 4x4, red-stained antlers left no question as to the caliber of buck we were looking at.

He would have easily scored 145 inches, probably closer to 150. Tiffany got her gun set in the shooting sticks and had him centered. At 80 yards the shot was a slam-dunk. But my instructions were to not shoot until I gave the okay, since I held the video camera as were trying to get footage for a TV show. This proves how difficult, and foolish, it can be to try to call and film a trophy blacktail buck, alone.

Just as I got on the buck and gave the okay, he turned, melted back into the wet scotch broom, blowing through his nose for the next ten minutes. It was one of the lowest points of my blacktail hunting career. Tiffany, head soaking wet from being pelted by the rain, just looked at me. No words were needed.

We hunted that area the next day and didn't see the buck. On the 17th consecutive day of hunting, and the last of the season, we split up. She dropped me off where we'd rattle in her buck, and she drove about eight miles to the west, to hunt another drainage.

When she picked me up that night, the blood on her hands said it all. She noticed the blood on my hands, too. Within five minutes of one another, we'd both taken blacktail bucks. Tiffany's was a fat 2x3, mine a little 4x4. Since it was the last day of the season, our goal was to put meat in the freezer. Mission accomplished.

Though neither of our bucks were record breakers, they were some of our most memorable ever taken. Why? It all comes down to the mental aspect of the hunt. For 17 days we devoted time to seriously trying to kill two big bucks. Though we each saw bucks bigger than what we ended up taking, we never fired a shot until the last few minutes in the final evening of the season.

Such is the sport of blacktail hunting. Often times persistence is rewarded, but just because you put in the time, don't feel that nature owes you a buck in return.

At the end of a blacktail seminar I once gave, I was approached by

a man in his late 30s. He was as excited about blacktail hunting as anyone I'd ever talked with. He'd been rifle hunting them and in the previous 13 years, hadn't filled a single tag. He could have shot smaller bucks, but was holding out for a big 4x4. In his mind, if he couldn't get a big buck, he'd rather go without. But what struck me most about this man was his knowledge of the deer, their behavior and his enthusiasm for the coming season. He had the type of mindset it takes to kill big bucks, and I'm sure, one day, he will.

Are you mentally prepared to meet the challenge of trophy blacktail hunting?

The mental aspect of hunting Columbia blacktails is different than with other big game. In sheep hunting, there are the mental rigors of big country to battle. In elk terrain, there's the mental and physical challenge of the hunt, followed by the work that follows once an animal is down. In mule deer country, there's the patient waiting game which involves glassing, covering ground, planning a stalk and bringing it all together in one perfect effort. In the world of whitetails, there come the mental games these cunning, secretive deer play. The mental world of blacktail hunting encompasses all of these factors, and more.

Never have I second guessed myself so much as when hunting blacktails. Is my tree stand in the right place? Is the wind really okay for me to stay in the ground blind? Am I rattling too loud or not loud enough? Should I push my luck and stalk closer to where I think the big buck's bed to be? After all my off-season scouting, what's to say the big buck I'd been seeing is still in the area? These are just a few of the questions that run through my mind on a regular basis when hunting blacktails.

However, despite the fact that I often question myself, every move I make in the woods is done so with forethought and confidence. I don't leave the house, plan a hunt or make a stalk unless I feel I can kill a buck. Over the years as I've hunted blacktails and other big game, I think the number one aspect that has helped me grow as a hunter is my self confidence. Bottom line, I expect to kill big animals when I go hunting, and I work as hard as I can to achieve this. I let no obstacles get in my way, and work year-round to prepare for that one shot.

In my early days, I went afield and hunted, not always with success. Though I didn't kill a lot of animals, I learned a lot. Today, I still learn something each time I'm in the field. I also apply much of what I've learned about blacktails and their behavior over the years, and as result, my hunts are more successful. It can be a different story if I'm searching for one particular trophy buck that's in the area. In this case, many times, if I don't see the big buck I want, I won't shoot one at all. Still, I open my eyes and mind to learning every single day I'm in the field, and I approach everything with the expectation to succeed.

So much of what we think we know about blacktails and their behavior comes down to speculation. That's because we rarely get to observe these secretive deer and really confirm what we think we know. Putting together every piece of the blacktail puzzle could well be one of the biggest challenges in all of North American big game hunting.

Overcoming these mental obstacles and having the confidence to believe in what you find, then bring it all together come hunting season, is what separates exceptional blacktail hunters from the rest. And the harder you work on a year-round basis, the more you'll learn.

I know of no other animal in the country where so much time can be devoted to figuring them out, without actually knowing what you're dealing with. This is where blacktail hunting separates itself from hunting other deer species. Big country, large tracts of public land, hunting pressure, changes in habitat and the inability to actually physically see a buck will test the heart of any hunter.

This is where the art of blacktail hunting turns to science. Come hunting season, our efforts are based on a hypothesis. That is to say, how we hunt comes down to what we know based on specific pieces of evidence we've accumulated over the course of the year, or several years. One thing I love about blacktail hunting, I learn more and more each year. The moment I stop trying to learn or start going through the motions, is the moment I have a reality check, regain my focus and start all over. It can be mentally draining, for my brain never stops working when blacktail hunting.

Much of the mental questioning which arises in the mind of blacktail hunters, is due to the fact that we're limited on hunting time. Often we only have a weekend, an evening or a morning before work to try and fill a tag. This leaves little time for guess work, and means we must be on top of our game if we wish to take a trophy buck in short order.

Not always are the moon phases ideal. Not always is the ground damp and quiet. Not always are the deer where we think they should be. The key is taking in all the information we've ever learned and bringing it all together to make the most sensible decision during the limited time we have to hunt.

Sometimes our efforts take many seasons to be rewarded. Other times it can happen quickly. If you head into the field and kill a big buck right away, stop and take note of what went in to that short hunt. Success didn't come by accident. You intentionally put yourself in to a position to hopefully kill a big buck, and it worked. Note everything that took place which directed you to be where you were. Pay attention to all the surroundings, and why a trophy buck was there.

Was it hunter pressure that drove him there? Was there a recent burn or logging operation which provided food? Which direction was the wind blowing, and how strong? What was the moon phase and what was the weather like in terms of fronts or pressure systems leading up to the hunt? What did the doe densities appear to be in the area? What was your exact elevation? Was the buck killed on a bench, in the bottom of a canyon or on a timbered ridge?

The more questions you can answer at the time you take a big buck, the more it will help you be successful in the future. One thing I have learned is that what attracts one trophy buck to an area is sure to attract another, and when a big buck is removed from a specific location, it doesn't take long for another to fill his spot.

Trophy hunting blacktail deer is a nonstop mental endeavor. Even in the off-season our minds are consumed with what deer are doing, and what we should be doing to help find success come hunting season. When you reach the point that blacktail deer induce a year-round mental hunting adventure, and get excited about living, eating and breathing the sport, then you're well on the way to becoming a trophy buck fanatic. At this stage, good things will start happening.

The Physical Game

One blacktail season I won't soon forget found me sitting in a ground blind 45 minutes before shooting light. I had a short walk from the truck – less than 300 yards – and it was easy, right down a logging road. Several trails and two drainages met where I had the blind set on the edge of a meadow.

Two hours into the hunt I drew my bow, put my sight pin behind the front shoulder of a buck at 28 yards and my hunt was over. The buck carried more than 130" of antler and on that day, I saw loads of deer, including a couple dandy bucks, one even bigger than the one I arrowed.

Though the buck was a real trophy, it was the ease of the hunt which I appreciated more than anything. I couldn't say this were it not for all my years of blacktail hunting, where grueling hikes, long days and sore body parts were the norm. No question, it's all those hard hunts I'd experienced over the years which really made me appreciate that easy hunt, which rarely happens, at least to me.

For me personally, I've found that the harder I work the more rewards I find. But that's not always the case. There are years when I've covered more ground than any hunter with common sense should, and failed to fill a tag. Then there are those years where all the off season works have been done, and come time for the hunt, I'm off exploring some other area instead.

45

The physical challenge faced by the trophy blacktail deer hunter takes on many facets. Much of what you experience comes down to the area you hunt. I know guys who take monster bucks year after year, all within five minutes of their homes, surprisingly close to suburban areas. This is an example of how big bucks find security among human populations, as long as that human isn't a hunter.

Suburban blacktail hunting can be physically easy, so too can valley floor blacktail hunting. Then again, hunting bucks in the lowlands can provide some of the most frustrating experiences a blacktail hunter could imagine.

Though the terrain is flat, physically speaking, in lowland blacktail haunts the dense brush can drive a hunter crazy. Here, bucks approached by hunters may lay tight to the ground, letting you walk within mere feet of them before bolting, if they choose to bolt at all. I've seen them lay with their chin flat to the ground and let hunters walk right by. It shows how bucks living in this habitat are dependent upon the foliage for cover.

In such settings, I've had my best success going into the area in the spring or summer and cutting shooting lanes near where tree stands will be placed. A tree stand greatly opens up the amount of land which can be seen in these brushy regions. Hit areas between a deer's feeding and bedding grounds, and hunt it early and late in the day, when the deer are moving to and from specific zones. The hope is to intercept a buck as it moves along a trail, through your shooting lane. I've had success doing this with bow, rifle and shotgun. Yes, even during gun season the brush can be too thick to shoot through, and doing some physical ground work in the off-season can make a big difference.

As you climb in elevation, blacktail hunts become more physically demanding. Bucks that live in the rugged Coast Range can be among some of the most challenging to hunt, both due to the thickness and the steepness of the terrain. Some of the toughest hunts of my life have been spent in the rugged Coast Range of northern California and the central Coast Range of Oregon.

In this big coastal country, still-hunting is the norm, but be pre-pared to cover lots of ground on foot. In areas where logging is still going on, glassing through a spotting scope can save lots of legwork. My preferred time to hunt the coastal region is in the middle of a rainstorm, or shortly thereafter. At these times the ground is quiet and tree limbs are often whipping in the wind, which offers the best chance of walking up on a buck. Because of the rigors involved with hunting this region, by the end of the day a hunter must prepare to be soaking wet from sweat on the inside, rain on the outside.

One thing the coastal blacktail hunter rarely has to worry about is snow, as the temperatures are usually relatively mild. Because of this, hunters can dress accordingly to be able to move through the woods quietly and comfortably. Many days I won't even wear rain gear when hunting the coast, for the noise is too much, and clothing with water-proof shells don't breath, meaning sweating and overheating become an issue. Progressing into the Cascade Range, hunts vary from moderate to intensely physical. The severity of the intensity comes down to where you hunt, and how hard you push yourself.

If you're a backcountry hunter, there are ways to access it: on foot and with horses. If hunting with horses or pack animals like mules, llamas or goats, prepare accordingly. This is big, serious country and knowing the animals you hunt with is as important as knowing the animals you hunt for.

Accessing the backcountry on foot is a whole different game. California's early archery season can get you into some major league country, as can Oregon's early High Cascade hunt and some of their late season muzzleloader hunts. Later archery seasons in Oregon and Washington, as well as some general gun areas throughout the blacktail's range, can also find you with the option of exploring as big of country as you'd care to. The key is being physically fit to do so.

If going into the high country, hunters will want to be physically ready and know their limitations. Some backcountry blacktail hunts can be made in a day, but to really learn the country and optimize your hunting time – especially late in the season when daylight hours are precious – it may be best to spend two or three days afield.

This means carrying a bivy or small tent, food and survival gear into the woods is necessary. Whatever you choose to pack, go light and keep in mind that the objective is to leave the woods with a dead deer. Being physically capable of doing this is a prerequisite to entering this challenging land.

Being able to field dress, skin, quarter, bone and cape your trophy buck is also important. This may sound trivial to some, but you'd be surprised at the number of "seasoned" hunters who don't know how to properly do these things.

Keep one thing in mind if you kill a buck in the backcountry, all meat must be brought out. This may require making two trips before it's all over, one for the deer, one for the camp. Then again, if you take a big enough backpack – internal or external frame, it depends on personal preference – and leave space, adding a boned-out buck to it for the journey out means you might be able to get everything out of the woods in one trip. Of course, that depends how heavy of a load you're capable of handling.

There's no substitute for being in top physical condition when hunting in rough territory. I'm not trying to play this off as a backcountry mule deer or elk hunt in the Rockies. It's not. It's blacktail hunting in the Cascades, but one thing that's important to realize – especially if you're a nonresident hunter – is just how big the Cascade Mountain Range truly is. Every season hunters and hikers die in these mountains, and most cases could have been avoided if the person knew just how big, rugged, demanding and foul-weathered, the region can be.

I know several serious blacktail hunters who work out year-round, lifting weights, running, biking and hiking. This is exactly what I do, and have done for years. My situation is a bit different from most hunters, however. Since I make my living by hunting, I want to be in the best physical shape I can to ensure top performance on the many hunts I go on throughout the year. When my schedule allows, I'll lift weights five times a week, and either run or hike three times a week.

What I do in the off-season sets the tone for the rest of the year, so I try to stay in shape year-round. Starting in January, I'll begin lifting weights and running. This carries into spring, until my schedule is interrupted by spring hunts in the West and abroad. By late spring I'm back on track, and regularly working out through the summer, until hunting season starts in mid-August.

Because my hunting season runs through the end of the year, it's important for me to have laid the ground work in the off-season, by lifting weights, running and getting my body into hunting condition. Once I hit the field in late summer, the daily hunting activities I carry out become my gym. From August through December I have no time to lift weights, and rely on daily physical outings in the woods to help keep me in shape, along with a healthy diet.

The cumulative efforts of working out and hunting will get the body in shape and can make a difference in the outcome of your blacktail season. If nothing else, the drive and personal ambition that I gain from working out provides me with the confidence and motivation to take my efforts in the field to another level, one I know I couldn't achieve without working out and eating right.

One thing I would encourage, if you're considering a high country blacktail deer hunt in the fall, is to make an effort to scout the area in the summer. This will allow you to gain an understanding of the exact physical demands that will be placed on you come hunting season, minus snow and freezing temperatures. It's also a great way to condition.

While hiking is a good way for hunters to reach the backcountry, there may be another option. With an ever-growing number of private timber companies locking their gates to keep out equipment vandals, many of them do allow access to the land behind gates as long as it's not in or on a motorized vehicle. This means walking and riding horses or mountain bikes can all be feasible ways to access prime, out-of-the way land.

The physical challenges of blacktail hunting can come in many forms.

49

Each season many big bucks are taken behind gated roads, where hunters have legally peddled their way into prime blacktail country. Bikes are far less maintenance than a horse, and are quieter, but you have to be in shape to handle it. Make sure that prior to the hunting season, your legs are in good condition and that your backside is used to spending some serious time on a bike seat. Upper body strength is also important for biking into and out of the blacktail woods. Simply put, no matter how you access your hunting grounds, there's no substitute for being in good shape.

Sitka blacktail deer are a different story. While these gorgeous blacktails are a thrill to hunt, they're not the toughest of deer to outwit. Still, their jet-black foreheads, stocky frame, stunning pelage and eyes that seem to slice right through you, make them one of the most enjoyable big game animals to pursue. The country in which Sitka blacktails dwell is also among the most striking on the planet. In fact, it's the country that should be the driving force behind the primary preparation of any Sitka deer hunt. If you're not prepared to tackle the country, not only can filling a tag become a concern, but so too can staying alive.

Some of my most dangerous hunts have taken place on Alaska's Kodiak Island, chasing Sitka blacktails. We've also had some grueling hunts amid the archipelago in southeast Alaska. The success of hunting deer in this unique blacktail habitat comes down to physical toughness and weather.

On one of my first hunts on Kodiak Island, we couldn't leave the boat for two days. We found the most protected cove we could tuck into, dropped anchor and didn't move the 42-foot vessel. We couldn't even launch the skiff to reach land so we could hunt, that's how dangerous the conditions were. The same happens to hunters every year, and they find themselves either stranded on a boat, in a tent or in a cabin or lodge.

During another hunt for Sitka blacktails, we got caught in an intense ice storm when we were on top of a mountain. We were forced to abandon our hunt and it was all we could do to get down off the mountain with our bodies and gear in-tact. What I would have given for crampons.

The earlier in the season you hunt Sitka blacktails, the better shape you need to be in for the higher you'll have to climb to find big bucks.

Even later in the year, if the snows haven't fallen, the big bucks won't drop toward the beaches. In this case, the only way to access them is on foot, which means being in prime shape.

I've seen several disappointed hunters in Alaska heading home with little forked-horns due to the simple fact they weren't in the physical condition required to hike up to where the big bucks were. There was no one or nothing to blame but themselves.

During an early December hunt one year, the conditions were perfect. Heavy snow was falling and the bucks were dropping fast in elevation. The rut was still going and deer were thick. On my first setup I rattled in a monster 4x4 that came running to the sound. I dropped him with one shot from the .300 magnum. He carried 108" of bone on his head, my best Sitka buck to date. The rest of the afternoon was spent packing, and we had high hopes of returning to the area the next day and finding bucks everywhere, as I had a second tag to fill.

When we woke up, the storm had passed, the temperature climbed more than 20° and the snow was melting fast. By that afternoon we had to climb nearly 2,000 feet, straight up, to find the big bucks. This is normal, where big bucks follow the snowline, whether it's dropping or receding.

No matter where you hunt blacktails, from Alaska to California or the high mountains to the ocean beaches, a key to consistent success is being physically prepared to do what's necessary to find deer. Based on a lifetime of hunting blacktails, and ever-increasing hunting pressure, it's my conclusion that the better shape a person is in, and the more they're willing to work during the hunt, the better their chance of success.

Sight & Sound

Deer have incredible senses. They must in order to stay alive. If they are not tuned in to what's going on around them, they risk death by predation. There is little room for error when it comes to deer letting down their guard, and hunters who are aware of this will consistently fill their tags. However, when it comes to a deer's vision and sense of sound, they may not be as good as you think.

While bowhunting one early season, I failed to see the bucks we'd been catching on trail cameras. One of the four bucks showed up, but where were the others? On day two of the hunt, I caught a whiff of something dead while sitting in my tree stand. Following my nose, it lead to a buck that had been killed by a cougar a few days prior, less than 100 yards from the stand. The fact a cat was in the area explained why bucks were not moving. I left, returned in the late season and filled my tag.

Nothing puts a buck on alert more than knowing predators are around, be they big cats or humans. But what do deer actually see and hear? The answer to that is based on speculation since it's impossible to actually get inside the brain of a deer. But science has come a long way, and certain studies have revealed eye-opening discoveries. Mind you, these studies have primarily been conducted on whitetails, at leading universities, but the general information applies to blacktail deer, too.

Keep in mind that with ever-changing environmental conditions, what a deer actually sees, hears and smells is highly situational. Winds, shadows, rain, snow, light and types of vegetation all impact the senses of a deer.

When it comes to sight, a deer's eyes are much like ours. That is, they see using a series of rods and cones. Deer have exceptional vision

Blacktails have incredible senses, and knowing how they see and hear will help boost success rates.

in low light settings, but they have only blue and green-yellow cones (humans have blue, red and green). This means a deer's color vision is lower in quality than humans, and their ability to differentiate certain hues is not as good.

Research has revealed that deer see blue colors very well, something to keep in mind when hunting in blue jeans. It's also been confirmed that deer don't see the color orange very well, meaning all those blaze orange caps and vests appear as shades of gray. What's even more important, deer have been found to be subpar at distinguishing detail. For example, a human with good visual acuity will have 20/20 vision. But deer have been proven to have only 20/100 vision, meaning they can't detect details like humans can.

I've seen this demonstrated many times while filming TV shows. Often times we'll have a hunter, two camera men toting tripods and giant cameras, and sometimes a guide, all following along into the woods. We have two rules: Move into the wind and when you see a deer, do not move. You'd be amazed to know how close we've gotten to deer, elk and antelope over the years, simply by knowing when and when not to move. Even when we call deer in, all of our gear – people and cameras – are in full view, but as long as no one moves, it's usually alright.

As long as you keep still and have on clothing that breaks up your outline, you're in good shape. Camo' patterns don't mean a thing to deer, only hunters. If it breaks up your outline, that's all you need.

During those times when a deer stares you down, and you're sure you've been busted, sit stone-still. It feels like the deer is actually looking through you at this point, for its trying to decipher what you are. In tense moments like these, avoid making direct eye contact with a deer, too. Often they'll go right back to feeding or walking along. Don't give up too early, for it's not over until they make a break for it.

Studies conducted at the University of Georgia – one of the country's leading deer study institutes – conclude that a deer's level of hearing is quite similar to that of humans. While deer are capable of hearing in the ultrasonic range, their hearing is most acute at moderate frequencies between 4,000 and 8,000 Hz. By comparison, humans hear best at between 2,000 and 5,000 Hz. Interestingly, a deer's best hearing range coincides with the frequencies of human voices, which is actually very close to those of many deer calls, including grunts.

While the above numbers indicate what a deer's inner ear is capable of, what about the outer ear? When you see the large ears of a deer pivoting like mini satellite dishes, they are simply trying to pinpoint where sounds are coming from. Their ears will help increase the level of sounds they take into their inner ear, and to prove this, simply cup your hands around the outside of each ear. By enlarging your outer ear with your hand, you'll see how deer rely on their big ears to help detect and channel sounds.

One thing this hearing information proves is that deer don't have highly sensitive levels of hearing humans often give them credit for. This means, when your calling or rattling, don't be afraid to get loud with it. I think this is one reason I've had such good success over my years of rattling – I don't hold anything back. Sounds don't carry well in the woods, especially when it's rugged and damp, as in most blacktail habitat. The louder you can be, the greater distance the sounds will carry.

Furthermore, if you're using high frequency sounds, you'll need to blow them especially loud. Calls like fawn and doe bleats are high pitched, and not easy for deer to detect. Likewise, grunt tubes that carry a lower volume, in the 3,000 to 4,000 Hz range will be better heard over higher toned calls.

Because deer are tuned in to lower pitch sounds, they can detect them at considerable distances. This means heavy footsteps, boots hitting on rocks or logs, clanging gear and slamming truck doors are all potential deer busters. In chapter 5, I'll detail my rattling and calling sequences, where much of my approach is based on a deer's sense of hearing.

By knowing what deer see and hear, hunters are better equipped to head into the woods and hunt wisely. Later, in chapter 5, I'll describe a deer's sense of smell, in the section on scent use and control.

Chapter Two
The Off Season
(January - June)

One thing that separates exceptional blacktail hunters from average ones is their level of dedication, even in the off season. In fact, to many folks, there is no such thing as an off season when it comes to blacktail deer. What defines the off season over that of the hunting season is the fact no weapons can be carried into the field in the off season. Other than that, there's still a lot a hunter can learn about deer this time of year.

For the definitive purpose of this chapter, the off season relates to the calendar months of January through June. During this time no hunting seasons are open, and deer are carrying out specific lifestyles which go through a series of intentional changes. Let's look at the blacktail's behavior during the off season, and see what hunters can learn based on the deer's actions and what's happening in their world. We'll also examine some of the activities hunters can carry-out during the off season to help increase their chance of success come hunting season.

Behavior & Scouting

During the months of January and February, blacktails lead a fairly sedentary life. Shortly after the rut, the objective of big bucks is to stay alive. This is the most vulnerable time of year for big bucks, for their fat reserves have been greatly depleted due to low food intake during the rut. If the winter is cold with lots of snow falling, the conditions become even more challenging for a buck to survive.

As the rut wraps up, bucks undergo a hormonal shift which causes them to lose their antlers. We'll talk more about hunting shed antlers in the following section. But what's important to know is that these deer likely drop their antlers very near where they were during the time of the rut. The sheds may also fall in the same place migratory deer have chosen to spend the winter. If the wintering grounds happen to be where the breeding takes place, all the better for hunters, as a lot can be learned here.

Being familiar with the six different subgroups of Columbia blacktails comes in handy this time of year. Resident bucks, like those found along valley floors, in the Coast Range and foothills of the Cascades, will usually drop their antlers near their core area, where they live year-round. Migratory blacktails and those that live in regions where they will move considerable distances to find does, often end up shedding their antlers far from where they spend the spring, summer and early fall.

Take for instance a Cascade blacktail. These bucks have been known to migrate several miles to reach their wintering grounds. The rut also takes place near many of these wintering areas, which means a higher concentration of big bucks occur here late in the fall or early winter. Come January, once the rut is well over, this means a high concentration of bucks will still be hanging in the area. This is the place hunters will want to return to in late January and February to search for antler sheds.

January and February are also some of the best times to scout for actual bucks. Generally, most blacktail hunts are done by early December, depending on which state you hunt in, with which weapon and in which unit. Once the hunts are done, the woods quickly clear of hunters, and they're not visited much again until the following hunting season. Hikers will enter into some of the blacktail's range during the summer months, but they pass through having caused little disturbance to the animals.

For hunters, all of January and February are prime times to be afield because the deer have relaxed and they are likely in the same area they were at the end of the hunting season. During these times the deer, both bucks and does, limit the amount of calories they burn. That means that when they feed, they choose their routes and food sources with care, so they can maximize their nutrient input and minimize their energy output.

Remember, these peak winter months are critical times for blacktails because very little of the food they eat has any substantial nutri-

56

tional value. This means they will not waste energy traveling long distances to seek nutritious foods that aren't there. Because a deer's movements can be so limited this time of year, this is a very good time to be in the field and learn where the core areas of a deer are, especially resident deer.

If targeting migratory bucks, note where they are and what routes they likely took to get there. This is a good time to physically locate deer and study topographic maps to learn what routes they likely took to arrive where they did. In addition to topo maps, local wildlife officials can be a great help when it comes to learning the migratory paths of specific blacktail populations. If your season ends before the migratory deer reach their wintering grounds, then the information you'll learn from seeing where the deer winter and figuring out the routes they took to get there will aid in determining where to hunt them the following season. Perhaps intercepting them early in their migratory movement is where you'll want to focus hunting efforts. You may be hunting them a few thousand feet higher than where they winter, and that can be confirmed on summer scouting missions.

When I'm out scouting this time of year, I look as eagerly for does as I do for bucks. Many times, especially when targeting resident bucks, it's the does that draw them to the area, and keep them there for a considerable time. If I can find good numbers of healthy does I know will be in the area next year, then I'll start looking for other signs of bucks. Remember, a blacktail doe can live up to 15 years. Find a doe's home and you'll find bucks.

Once I've located does, if I'm not physically seeing bucks I'll look for other signs. The most important signs I'll look for are rubs. If I can find fresh rubs made from the recent rut, then my attention has been captured. But what really gets me excited is when I find new rubs, with old rubs on the surrounding trees. Many of the best areas I hunt have rubs on the trees from the previous three, four or five consecutive years, even longer.

In some of these areas I keep track of when specific rubs were made, and check every winter to see what new ones have been added. If rubs are present year after year in an area, then I know there is a stable population of does around, as well as bucks. In some of the lower elevation areas where I've pulled some big bucks out of over the years, DHLS has wiped out the does. In these areas, it's been years since I've found a fresh rub. This is valuable information to know, and it can be acquired in the off season rather than wasting valuable time during a day's hunting in the fall to figure it out.

From January through March, whenever snow falls in the blacktail woods, I try to get out and scout as much as possible. This is especially true in the valley floor areas, the lower elevations of the foothills of the Cascades, in the Coast Range and within some of the open country I hunt. Some of these places only receive snow once every few years, if that.

Snow can be a great learning tool, for several reasons. First, blacktail hunters rarely get the luxury of patterning blacktail movement based on tracks, and snow provides the perfect platform on which to do this. Because blacktails live in habitat where it's hard to decipher their tracks, other than along well-used trails, it can be tough trying to figure out how many deer are in an area.

Once snow falls, get out and scout. Often times the snow doesn't stick around long at the lower elevations, so if you can take a morning off work, do it. What you can learn in a few hours will be worth it.

Another reason snow is a valuable learning tool is because it allows bedding areas to be discovered. One thing that will amaze you is how often blacktails get up, feed and re-bed during the course of a day. Even in winter, where their movements are limited, you'll be surprised at how often they bed. You'll also be able to see where they bed, and figure out why.

When snow covers the ground, make it a point to get out and search for deer sign.

58

Once you've found a fresh bed, try to conclude what time of day it was used and try to determine why the deer bedded where it did. Study wind direction, which way the deer was facing, what it used as a protective backdrop, where it last fed and which direction it got up and moved to, as well as how long it may have bedded (this can often be evidenced by how much snow melted due to the deer's body heat).

Also, study the tracks closely on these snowy days. There will be a more detailed look at blacktail tracks in Chapter 4, but when it snows, it's the best time to get out and see how many deer are in the area based on their tracks. Bucks usually leave a bigger print than a doe, but not always, and this can be hard to decipher in some snow conditions. In deeper snow, bucks seem to drag their hind legs more than does, so look for this.

Once found, follow tracks to see where they lead. No doubt, if you stick with them long enough you'll find the deer. See where the tracks lead and ask yourself why. This time of year you'll likely be on a south facing slope, where deer can optimize what sun rays make it to earth. Look to see how high up the ridge a buck goes to bed. Did the buck go higher than the rest of the animals? Has the buck already split off by himself? Have smaller bucks started forming bachelor groups yet?

If on doe tracks, follow them to their beds and see how they situate themselves when they lay down. How close are they to one another? What direction are each of them facing and why? These are just some of the questions that, when answered now, in the off season, can pay dividends come hunting season.

As snows melt and photoperiods lengthen with the approach of spring, big bucks will start retreating to their more comfortable core areas. For migratory bucks, this means moving to higher ground. For nonmigratory bucks this may mean very little movement at all, or maybe a slight shift into an area that will soon be greening up with herbaceous and grassy foods. During March through April, I don't do a lot of active scouting. Instead, I let the deer go about their daily routines, undisturbed.

From the start of May through June, however, I'm out as often as I can be. Whether it's an intentional scouting trip or observations I make as I'm out chasing spring turkey or bears, this time of year I'm looking for two things: does and fawns. If the does have no fawns with them, I check to make sure they're plump and pregnant. There location this time of year is where they will drop their fawns, so I make it a point to keep track of them.

Once I've located several pockets of does, I continue checking the areas to see when the fawns drop. If you're unable to scout some of the areas you hunt, May and June are good months to talk with loggers, ranchers, farmers as well as Forest Service and wildlife personnel to learn if they are seeing newborn fawns. By knowing when the fawns hit the ground, you can back up about 200 days and see when the rut took place. Such information can be invaluable, for even if you don't hold a tag which can be used during the rut, you'll gain insight as to when bucks will start pre-rutting in your hunting areas.

Starting in June, I'll begin searching for bucks. Now their antlers have amassed some growth to the point you can just about predict how big they'll be come late August, when the velvet is usually shed. Not only will I be looking for big bucks, but I'll also be trying to figure out how many bucks made it through winter. I'll also be studying pelts, to see if any deer, bucks or does, have been hit with DHLS.

From July 4th to the season opener – usually the last part of August or the first part of September – I'll try and get out as frequently as I can to search for trophy bucks. In these early summer months bucks will be feeding on a variety of herbaceous life, and will spend a great deal of time feasting on blackberry bushes. It's around these food sources that I'll spend the majority of my scouting time.

The winter and spring months are not only enjoyable times to be afield, but a great deal can be learned about blacktails and their population dynamics at this time. It's also a good time to learn the carrying capacity of the habitat you hunt, which will be a solid indicator of just how many bucks should be in the area.

For more accurate population index estimations in terms of the buck to doe ratios in your hunting areas, check with regional biologists to see what their latest studies show. These ratios can greatly vary from area to area. One thing you'll discover is that it's tough, even for biologists, to get a solid population count on blacktails simply because of the dense habitat they call home. But you'll also learn that the more help you can get from folks like this, the more information you'll learn about the animals and areas you hunt.

Antler Shed Hunting

Shed antler hunting is usually carried out for three main purposes. First, it allows hunters to learn about the bucks in the area in hopes of increasing success rates come hunting season. Second, it's a fun way to spend time, either alone, with a dog or with the family. Third, sheds can be found and sold to collectors or artists.

For years, hunting for shed antlers has been a common pastime of mule deer and whitetail hunters. Mule deer hunters spend numerous hours scouring the snow-covered winter range, hoping to find antler sheds that will tip them off to the true genetic potential the bucks are capable of reaching in the areas they hunt. Whitetail hunters back east have been covering small sectors of land for decades, hoping to reveal clues about the bucks that live in the lands they hunt.

But when it comes to hunting for blacktail antler sheds the playing field changes. For these deer, dense brush, steep, giant hillsides, big timber, vast rolling hills, riparian and deciduous tree lines, and jungle-like river bottoms characterize the land where time is spent searching for antlers. As with hunting the deer themselves, looking for their ant-

Sheds reveal a great deal as to the caliber of bucks in an area, and where bucks live or migrate to. A match to this shed would have seen a rack scoring over 140".

61

lers is a true challenge. Furthermore, the methods of approach can be dictated by the land itself, making the challenge even more taxing.

The key to remember is that shed antlers are a resource for the hunter and must be properly understood and utilized in order to be effective. For instance, if you hold an early season deer tag, knowing where sheds are found each winter won't do much good unless you're hunting lower elevation, home-body bucks. If, however, the area you hunt late in the season holds migratory deer, then time needs to be spent searching for sheds amid their wintering grounds. Correlating the time of season you intend to hunt with the buck's location during the time they shed their antlers is crucial.

For some hunters, it's an accomplishment to find a few sheds a year. For others, the dynamics of shed hunting is changing, and they're finding up to two dozen sheds a day. Some are doing it through hard work, on foot. Others are finding how valuable dogs can be.

In this section we'll take a close look at the options for and strategies of hunting blacktail antler sheds. Taken into account will be the varied terrains these deer live in, as well as the difference in hunting nonmigratory bucks versus migratory ones.

In one of the areas I've been blacktail hunting in recent years, I spent three days looking for sheds in late February. I found nothing. On day four I started laying a grid on a south facing slope I'd not yet covered. I was near the top of the hill, on the edge of a small, grassy meadow. There was a stand of 30 year old timber above it, a mix of conifers and deciduous trees below it, with grassy meadows in between and a creek in the bottom of the drainage. On that day I found four good blacktail sheds, and was elated. The next fall I returned to the area in late October, toward the end of the general rifle season, and took a good 4x4 less than 100 yards from where I picked up those sheds. One of the sheds was his.

Though I was hunting for these sheds on foot like I always have, the fact that my efforts paid off and were rewarded with a good buck is all that mattered to me. Soon after this, I learned about using dogs to hunt for blacktail sheds.

The use of dogs to help find shed antlers is something I'd heard about for years. Usually people would grab their black lab and head into the blacktail woods in hopes of finding antlers. It worked, and still works, but there's a new breed of shed hunters and new breeds of dogs being used with astounding success to root-out blacktail sheds. Simply put, hunting for shed antlers is one of the fastest growing crazes among blacktail hunters, and dogs are playing a huge roll in the right situations.

I took the time to visit with and learn from good friend Steve Waller, owner of Cabin Creek Kennels in western Oregon (www.cabincreekgundogs.com). Steve has been training dogs since about 1970, and his level of knowledge and dedication to the sport is impressive. What he's been doing with dogs and antler shed hunting has revolutionized how people are searching for antlers, especially blacktail hunters. Following are important pieces of advice Steve shared with me.

Many hunting breeds of dogs can be trained to retrieve antlers. Labradors are what Steve started working with, and they do a good job, but he found the strain of running hillsides for hours, especially in the summer, really tired them out. However, there are many hunters who use Labs in the winter and early spring, when temperatures are cooler, and do great with them.

The Ferraris of hunting dogs for antler sheds, Steve has discovered, are Pudelpointers, a standard poodle-German pointer mix. These dogs are very athletic, sleek and can really cover ground. Their level of stamina is exceptional, and they are willing to work hard, exactly what's necessary in the rugged terrain of most blacktail habitats.

Waller has worked with many breeds of dogs, and up until now finds Pudelpointers to be best suited for hard-core, serious trophy deer hunters. He advises the importance of getting a pup from a breed that has a lot of hunting and retrieving desire in it, and from what he's found, the Pudelpointer is the most natural when it comes to finding antlers.

It's interesting, in parts of Europe, antlers have been used to train dogs for years. This is because dogs can be utilized to hunt deer in many places over there. They've been working Pudelpointers for a long time, and here, in the West, this breed seems to be a natural.

Generally, when they're working in the field, upland dogs get their heads up in the air, thus are able to scent things a long ways away. In a good, low-wind, these dogs can smell chukars 300 yards out. The same with the antler sheds; dogs that hunt with their heads up will detect more scent, especially in brushy canyons where blacktails live. They'll also wind more mule deer sheds in sage country, as well as elk antlers in big country.

When it comes to training your dog to hunt for antler sheds, Waller suggests beginning early. Start them on antlers as soon as you get them home. Give them antlers for a short time period, making sure they don't chew it to pieces. It's not a play toy; make the antlers something special for the dogs to associate with.

As for the actual training, ideally the pup should be six months of age or older. It should be house-trained as well as introduced to the environment it will be hunting in. Until they're six months old, let the puppy be itself. Teach them basic commands; sit, stay, etc., and don't be too hard on them. If the pup makes mistakes, so what. This is their time to learn, and your time to bond with them.

After about six months to a year, once their adult teeth come in and depending on how they mature, it's time to teach them to force fetch. Force fetching is using an act of stimulation to cue a dog to pick up an object on command and reliably return it to the person in charge.

It's not necessary to force fetch with antlers if your dog will be a bird dog, too. But if your number one purpose of having the dog is to find antler sheds, then you will want to teach them to force fetch with antlers. Here's why, notes Waller. "Say your dog gets in a canyon, grabs an antler, and something else like a grouse gets their attention. They might drop the antler and you'd never know it was there. For devoted antler shed hunters, force fetching on antlers can remedy this, and is very important.

According to Waller, your next step is to start training your dog to handle, or cast-off. This is the basic hand signal that teaches your dog to move on command. If you've got your dog to force fetch, that's the hard part, now the fun begins in the training process.

When teaching your pup to handle or cast-off, Waller likes to use what he calls the baseball drill, with the pitcher's mound being where you start off your pup with the command, "over" for 1st and 3rd base, "back" for 2nd base.

As your pup starts to handle, you can begin running him to piles, which is a pile of bumpers placed in the field. For antler shed hunting purposes, replace the standard bumpers with a pile of antlers. This will help the dog learn what to look and smell for when it's time to hit the woods. Start at 30 yards, have him heel and send him to the pile and back with a retrieve to hand.

Waller suggests you avoid training your pup more than 10 or 15 minutes at a time, as they get bored and lose focus easily. Also, make sure they don't chew on the antlers. Always try to stop on a positive note, when your pup is doing well.

The key is taking the time to get your new pup into the field as much as possible. Remember, everything is new to them, and in their first season, it's worth taking the extra time to spend quality days, one-on-one with them in the field. If you're new to the world of dog training, don't be overwhelmed with the few basic steps highlighted here. If starting out in your, or the dog's, first year, these steps can help shape things in the direction you want them to go.

The biggest decision you'll likely have to make is whether or not you want to solely train your dog on antlers or incorporate working with birds, too. This decision really depends on what people want. Some guys are hard-core shed hunters, especially when it comes to blacktails and Roosevelt elk. These folks are asking dogs to do a lot, something they must be taught and disciplined to do. For instance, if you expect your dog to go a few hundred yards into the bottom of a deep canyon and search for antlers, they must be taught how to do this, and using antlers to educate them is the best way.

If they bring up a big antler, then you can go down into the canyon, work it thoroughly

Dogs are becoming very popular in the world of antler shed hunting, and with good reason.

65

with your dog, and usually find the match. For a trophy hunter, the use of dogs is an efficient way to learn where big bucks hang out. Even if you do train a dog heavy on antlers, that's not to say they won't hunt birds. Most will, it's their instinct and that's why it's important to invest in a dog with a good pedigree. For serious deer hunters, you just might want to focus more on antlers, since that's something they have to be taught to look for.

Once you do hit the woods with your dog, the key to maximizing the number of antler sheds you find is getting into the field when the scent is still strong of blood and bone. The more fresh the antler shed, the more likely the dog is to pick up its smell. The longer a shed antler lies in the woods, the more it looses odor, making it tougher for even the best of dogs to detect.

Late January through February are considered the prime months for antler shed hunting. This is when the deer are shedding their antlers, and the sooner you can be in the field after an antler is shed, the better the chance of the dog finding it. Then again, you may want to wait until March to do your searching. Here's why.

If the deer in your area are sensitive to human pressure or dogs, you don't want to go in before they've dropped their antlers and risk spooking them out of there. If it's a little honey-hole you know other hunters likely won't find, then it may be in your best interest to wait until early or mid-March, when you know all the bucks have dropped their antlers, and then go in. If migratory bucks are your target deer on late season hunts, the last thing you want to do is drive them out of their small core area before they drop their racks. In this case, waiting until March is a good idea.

Weather conditions play a huge part in a dog's ability to hunt shed antlers. Waller feels the best conditions are when it's overcast, but dry and not too hot so the dog doesn't get tired out. Better yet, if there's a very light wind lying down on the ground, then the chances of the dog picking up a scent is better; it's pretty much the same as with upland bird hunting. This will keep scent low to the ground, and with the dogs working into the wind, they'll locate a lot more antlers. In these conditions, Labs' work great, for it's not too stressful on their bodies.

If it's too wet, like during or after heavy rains, it can mask the scent of the antler. If it's too dry, the scent can dissipate into the air, making it tough for even a dog to locate. In the coastal or brush country habitats of blacktails, the antlers could have fallen beneath heavy cover, and it's important to have good conditions to help get that scent into the air. The more favorable the conditions, the more ground a dog can efficiently cover.

Waller is hearing reports from guys he's trained dogs for, and they are bringing home 50-70% more antlers than when they hunted them alone, on foot. What's even better, they're going into these same areas during hunting season and scoring on monster, record book bucks.

Another benefit of hunting for antler sheds; you can involve the whole family this time of year. It's a great way to teach kids about animal behavior and get the entire family in the outdoors.

The dedicated antler hunter looking to use the best dog, and find the most antlers, can greatly increase their odds of success come hunting season. It boosts your confidence just knowing there are trophy animals in the area, and if you hang your stands in the right place, or still-hunt the same area where you found big sheds, the chance of tagging that record book animal dramatically increases.

But what if you don't have the time, money or desire to invest in a dog for hunting antler sheds? You can still do it the old fashioned way, on foot. In fact, many people still prefer searching for antlers on foot, for many reasons. Tranquility is one. The sense of accomplishment is another. Some don't want to risk spooking deer out of the area when their searches begin early, say in January and February, when migratory bucks may still be in the area.

There are some seriously dedicated blacktail shed hunters out there, and one of the best I know is Steve Holte. Steve lives in southwest Oregon, amid what's likely to be the best trophy blacktail hunting grounds on the planet.

I've chatted with Steve on many occasions and he's taught me a lot about hunting shed antlers. Steve doesn't own a quad or motorcycle, and chooses to hunt antlers on foot, even though he has to walk more than a mile back in to his favorite spots.

One of the first things Steve looks for is an area where oak trees and buckbrush grow together. Steve acknowledges the fact he does live in a unique blacktail region, but believes that if hunters study their area closely and know deer movements, anyone can find sheds. Steve targets migratory bucks, and hunts during Oregon's late season which encompasses the rut.

Steve looks for the oak and buckbrush mix, as he's observed the deer still eating on oaks this time of year, even if there aren't any acorns. He's also noted that the deer seek out the middle-age buckbrush as a main winter food in the area. Steve says that 60% of the sheds he finds are in these open areas.

Keeping in mind a buck's core area shrinks because he's not moving much after the rut, Steve also spends lots of time on benches. He tries to find a core area that offers what the bucks need, namely a little feed, shelter and some water. Most of the antlers he finds are about two-thirds the way up a ridge, usually near a bedding area or in a transition zone on a steep hill where they drop when the deer are moving through.

Steve advises hunters to focus on the southern exposures, not necessarily the southern slopes. Interestingly, his favorite spots are slopes that run to the west and receive southern sun exposure, as he believes this optimizes food growth.

Trail cameras are an important tool for blacktail shed hunters.

Over the years Steve has learned to hunt smart. His shed hunting routine used to be, come home from work, put the kids to bed, and then head out with a flashlight to begin his search. Today, he's learning the areas better, and learning a great deal about the deer, thanks to trail cameras.

"Now I just concentrate on one good spot where I know big bucks gather," Steve shares. The last time I'd spoken with Steve he'd caught 17 different bucks on trail cameras and had found at least one side of the antlers from 10 of those bucks. "One thing trail cameras do is reveal what deer are in the area. Then, when I find an antler, I can confirm it's the same buck."

Because Steve targets migratory deer, he waits until late February to start scouting for sheds, so as to make certain he doesn't spook bucks out of the area. One thing he advises: "If there's a delicate area where you think they might be spooked, wait for the deer to move out before going in and looking for sheds. If it's a secluded area that you don't have to worry about other people finding, wait as long as possible, to allow the deer to move out at their leisure."

Between all his hunting, trail trimming and shed scouting, Steve may enter an area 30 or more times, so he gets to observe a lot. "I've always heard that does get the prime feed," he notes, "but I've not seen this. I think the big bucks get what they need first, then the does. I also think trophy bucks will tolerate a certain number of deer in their core area, and when this number gets too high, they run deer out, especially insubordinate bucks."

In some of Steve's favorite hunting grounds, he's been picking up sheds in the same place for 15 years. One thing he's learned is that the bucks drop their racks about the same day every year, in almost the same spots. He has matching sets of sheds off one buck from nine consecutive years. Sometimes it may take him months, even years, to find the match. Some matches will never be found.

If you're a bowhunter or hunt the last few days of rifle season, Steve believes shed antlers can help you find success when migratory deer are your target. "The sheds give you lots of information about the area you hunt. Their core area might not be exactly where you find sheds, but the bucks travel through areas where sheds are found, and this will help you figure out how to effectively hunt the land. If you find sheds in areas where you hunt later in the season, you'll have a chance of killing that buck."

Sheds also teach you about the number of bucks in an area, and how big they really are. They also keep you optimistic for what you might find, which is huge, mentally speaking.

Steve suggests that when you start looking for sheds, concentrate on areas with sign. "Look for rubs, tracks, trails, feeding areas, anything that will give you a clue to where deer hang out. Don't waste time in heavy brush areas or too wide-open of meadows, as most of the sheds will be on the fringes of where brushy country meets the open lands."

Steve's final words of advice, "If hunting the early season, either archery or rifle, don't waste time hunting where the sheds of migratory bucks are found. The bucks won't be there that time of year."

When it comes to hunting for resident deer sheds, another accomplished shed hunter, Chris Toy, has that figured out. Chris lives only a couple miles from me, and concentrates on hunting foothill blacktails. These are pure blacktail, and he prefers covering country on foot to find his sheds.

Chris Toy found the sheds of this big buck, set up in the right spot, and arrowed the 150" buck in Oregon's early bow season.

70

On Chris's last shed hunting season, he found 67 total sheds, 14 of which were complete sets. One of these sheds is bigger than the 150-inch buck he arrowed two seasons prior, a buck that fell 400 yards from where he found his sheds the winter before.

The land Chris hunts is hilly, with lots of Douglas fir trees, some big timber, a mix of small oak thickets, some logged units nearby and loads of thick brush in the many draws and valleys. Like Steve, Chris also finds many sheds from the same buck in the same area, some within 50 yards of one another from year to year. He also uses trail cameras to monitor the deer, as well as internet websites which provide aerial images of the country.

One thing that Chris has learned is how many bucks really are out there. He points out, "I've lived my whole life in this area, and not until I started hunting for sheds did I realize how many bucks there are out there, and big bucks!"

Chris no longer wonders through areas hoping to stumble upon sheds. His efforts are focused and he's finding more sheds now than ever. By past experience, and also downloading and studying aerial images such as those found at www.map.live.com, Chris knows exactly where he wants to go. He'll even get waterproof paper and print aerial images on to that, so he can take it into the field for a reference. This tool has single-handedly helped him find lots more sheds and more deer during hunting season.

While shed hunting in the foothills of the Cascades, Chris spends nearly all his time scouring the south facing slopes. Sometimes, when the habitat looks perfect, he'll search the southwest facing slopes, especially if it's exposed enough to catch a bit of afternoon sunlight during the months he looks for sheds.

Chris is a bowhunter, and though these are resident deer he's after, he doesn't want to risk spooking them from their small wintertime core area. "I'll start looking for antlers in the middle of February," shares Chris. "I'll hit every little oak clearing I can find, and spend most of my time around the fringes."

Chris could wait and go later, maybe in March, when all the bucks have dropped their antlers, but he likes starting earlier for two reasons. First, other hunters are in the area, and he wants to beat them to it. Second, he's convinced the biggest bucks drop their antlers first.

Scouting efforts can continue into the spring, but by then, many antlers get lost in high grass. This might be where the use of dogs can come in handy, after the ground has been covered on foot and the deer have expanded their core areas.

Chris stresses that though he does find most of his trophy class sheds up high on the ridges, he also finds a surprising number of big sheds down low. He also finds them along the edges of the smallest clearings. He carefully records where he finds each shed, and on what day. Over the years he's found a consistent pattern to when and where mature bucks shed their antlers.

No doubt, hunting for antler sheds can greatly increase your actual trophy blacktail hunting success. The key, however, is knowing the type of bucks you're after, resident or migratory, then figuring out how to best find their sheds. Correspond the time of season you hunt with the deer and the habitat they occupy, and you'll discover the benefits of hunting antler sheds.

Map Research

The off season is a good time to start studying the area you'll be hunting, without setting foot in the field. While attending college, I majored in geography at the University of Oregon, which at the time had the top geography department in the country. Of course, my motives were hunting-based, which was not the norm for those enrolled in the program. What I learned in those years is still invaluable to me and my hunting success.

Of all the geographical tools a hunter has at their disposal, topographical maps and three-dimensional photographs are likely the most important. In the growing age of technology, computers have changed our world, and this is also true for hunters looking to learn more about the land they hunt, or would like to hunt.

There are various internet sites which can help hunters learn about the land, and three have helped me. The first is called EarthExplorer and is offered by the United States Geologic Survey (USGS). This program provides recent, high-quality aerial photos that are taken on a five to seven year cycle and covers all of the United States.

Ariel photos for EarthExplorer come from various sources, including the International Space Station, space shuttles, Skylab, Gemini and Apollo missions, dating back from 1965 to the present. The digital images of aerial photos combine the image characteristics of the photos with geo-referenced qualities of a map.

To learn more about a hunting area, simply go to the website, www.usgs.gov and type in EarthExplorer in the search box. Then, various addresses will appear on the screen. Click on earthexplorer.usgs.gov/, which will then take you to the main EarthExplorer site. From there, a digital image of the world will pop up. Just click on the area you wish to take a closer look at, and keep enlarging the image.

Eventually you'll be able to zoom in on the area and see what the foliage and terrain is like. By putting the cursor on the image, clicking and holding it down, you can move the actual map around to see the entire area in detail.

There's also a "terrain" button, which will show lines of relief whereby allowing you to more closely study the steepness of the land. The more you zoom in on the terrain feature, the more pronounced and defined the lines of relief become. What's great, the terrain reliefs are broken down into layers of tints, contours and contours with shading. These are great ways to give an accurate portrayal of the land.

Satellite images and aerial photographs can also be purchased from the USGS. Talk about technological advancements. Now you can study these three-dimensional objects in the comfort of your own home. Back in my college days, I spent many hours in the geography building studying black and white 3D-ariel shots through antiquated lenses. It worked, but today's color shots of the land are much nicer.

One of the most amazing on-line geography aids is Google Earth. To access this program, enter a search for Google Earth. This will take you to a page where you can download the latest version of Google Earth, for free. Once downloaded, view the free tutorial that's offered, as this will teach you how to use the system. It's easy, and takes only a few minutes. But be warned, once you're set, you'll spend hours researching all your hunting grounds. I've used this program to explore hunting areas all around the world, it's incredible.

What Google Earth provides is a three-dimensional look at the land, from both an above angle as well as a ground level view. One thing I really like about this program is the Swoop Navigation system. With your mouse, it's easy to use the navigation controls at the top of the photo page to swoop in from outer space, all the way down to ground level. Another great tool is the "sunlight" feature. To view the sunlight feature, click on the icon at the top of the photo page of the area you're exploring. Then move the time-slider bar to the time of day you want to see. I find this to be very beneficial when trying to see when and where afternoon and morning shadows will appear and disappear. When trying to learn about deer's feeding areas and travel routes, the sunlight feature can help you figure out when and where you need to be.

There are three navigation controls in the upper right hand corner of your target page. The top one, called the "look" joystick, allows you to look around the area in a 360° view from where you are standing. The next one, called the "move" joystick, allows you to move from one place to another. I like this one when exploring mountain ranges and valleys, as it allows you to get a true feel for what the country is like. The final control is called the "zoom slider," which allows you to swoop down to ground level and back out again. Though the image you zoom in on flattens out as you get closer, as you move across the landscape high and low elevation marks can still be seen. Be careful not to zoom in too closely when moving around with your zoom slider as you will lose some continuity.

At the bottom of each image you bring up on Google Earth, latitude and longitude coordinates are clearly displayed. Also, the elevation is displayed and it actually changes, or calculates, as you travel across the landscape. Finally, the date and time the images were taken appears.

The third online imaging aid can be found at www.map.live.com. I like the clarity of their images for basic landscape scouting. The imagery also seems to be updated.

Keep in mind that these websites are meant to show you pictures of the real world. Some images are sharper than others, and some are pixilated a bit more than others when you're zoomed in. As technology continues to advance, watch for these and other programs to improve. There are some sites which, if you pay to become a member, provide higher resolution and more up-to-date images.

Though modern technologies of mapping are a luxury, I still view them with my topography maps along side. This is because the digital photos, though they are excellent for judging the size of the country, age class of trees and vegetation, shadow movement and much more, still don't provide the overall relief indicated on a topo map. EarthExplorer comes close to doing this, but topo maps can still reveal important clues that benefit hunters, besides simple relief lines.

Topo maps can be picked up at various sporting goods stores, or on-line. Just type in "topo maps" as a web-search and you'll be blown away at what comes up, not only in the form or topo maps, but websites which offer more aerial views of the world. Topo maps are excellent sources when laid next to Bureau of Land Management (BLM), Forest Service and Fish & Wildlife maps. Private timber companies may also provide maps of their areas.

Many backcountry hunters consider topo maps to be among the most valuable of all hunting aids. But the information you look to get out of a topo map depends on the area you plan on hunting. The more remote and rugged the terrain to be hunted, often times the more beneficial a topo map tends to be. Then again, if you're simply looking for logging road or hiking trail access, springs, drainages and other such common features, then a topo map can benefit you, too. Keep in mind that not all maps capture everything, including spring sources.

If hunting high, broken terrain, try to identify big draws, basins and canyons on the topo maps. Look to see what the percentage of timberland is compared with open terrain – somewhere between 50-75% timbered land is what some hunters go by as this offers good glassing opportunities while at the same time providing ample cover and likely food sources for deer populations in those areas. You might also want to locate trail heads, to see where hunting pressure is most likely to come from. The more trails leading into an area, and the more easily they are accessed, the more hunters you'll have to contend with.

In the area where I live, recreational backpacking is very popular, the norm for a lot of breathtaking blacktail terrain. Some of the more valuable resources out there for hunters looking to access and learn about backcountry blacktail land are trail guides and destination-type backpacking books.

Other good mapping sources that can help you learn more at home as well as when you're in the field are Global Positioning Systems (GPS) that come with topo map features, or have the ability to download topo map features. Also, there are some impressive computer programs out there which can be plugged in, whereby allowing you to learn about the topography of the land you want to hunt.

While we're on the subject of satellite imagery, it's worth taking a look at what can be learned from wildfires. It's no secret that some of the best blacktail habitat is that which is created by wildfires. Especially in drier areas, wildfires enhance a great deal of habitat by making room for new growth to occur. Satellite photos of these fires can give hunters a big advantage when it comes to figuring out where to hunt.

There are too many website-based, fire map resources to list, but hunters can access valued information on current and even past burns. Suffice it to say all you need to do is type in a specified web search, and then go from there. It's as simple as entering: "Images of wildfires burning in northern California," or wherever you want to research, and letting the links lead you. Agencies such as NASA, the US Forest Service, state Forest Service and more, regularly post incident reports on new fires. You can also find images on fires from previous years.

From there you can download the images, print them off, and take them afield. Keep these files on hand and refer to them two to five years after they occurred – depending on how fast the new growth comes back in the specific area – and start hunting. Big bucks will find these new, nutritious food sources, and fire maps can help you find the deer. I know of some hunters in northern California who feel these are some of the most underutilized tools available to hunters.

On their own, all of these tools can be beneficial to the hunter looking to learn more about the terrain to be hunted. Combining multiple forms of these resources provides even more complete information which can help improve the outcome of your hunt. Once you conduct map research and tie it in with satellite images, and start killing big bucks because of it, you'll realize the value of these pieces of information.

Food Plots

Food plots and blacktails; mention the two together among a crowd of avid blacktail hunters and you're likely to receive as many different looks as there are people. Part of this has to do with the fact food plots are commonly associated with whitetails. Part of it has to do with the fact most blacktail hunting takes place on public land, in big country, where food plots aren't even an option. Part of it comes down to the morals of it all; should blacktail hunters stoop so low as to integrate food plots into their hunting scheme?

Food plots – or nutritional supplements, whatever you want to call it – do several things, two of which are important for hunters. First, they attract deer to an area. Second, they allow bucks to grow bigger antlers. But food plots do much more than that. In areas where DHLS has made an impact, food plots have provided valued sources of nutrients to help get more deer through winter. Food plots also provide very nutritious foods that help does prepare their bodies for motherhood.

Overall, food plots can greatly increase the health of a blacktail population, whereby simultaneously allowing their true genetic potential to be maximized. Within the expressed traits of bigger racked bucks, does are every bit as important for proper breeding and further producing healthy, quality deer over the long-term. In terms of big antler production, some of the genetically superior does are every bit as valuable as bucks, since they are 50% of the breeding equation. Maybe nutritional supplements can help, as they do make sense in certain situations.

If you stop and think about it, food plots do have a place in the world of some blacktail hunters. The key word here is some, not all. This is where the benefits of recognizing the six different faces of blacktails comes in handy; and that's the overall purpose of this book, to help all blacktail hunters, no matter where, how or when they hunt.

So, in what places do food plots have applicability in the world of blacktail hunting? Obviously food plots can be helpful on private lands. No matter what their location or elevation, private land food plots can make a difference in your hunting. If you own or lease blacktail property, food plots can be utilized, should you choose to do so. Public ground food plots are normally restricted to government agencies, timber companies, hunting organizations, and so on, and if done properly, you won't even know they're there.

The first time I put in supplementary feed, I tilled up about 1/4-acre of land and planted it with white clover in the spring (I later learned this wasn't the best choice). By fall the clover grew and deer came to it in big numbers. In fact, I was blown away with how many blacktails feasted on the clover. By winter the clover went dormant, and my travels took me away from the property and the attention it needed. Due to my neglect, the food plot was taken over by weeds and grass. I need to get going on another plot, and do it right this time.

There are many thoughts and theories when it comes to implementing a blacktail food plot, and most ideas are based on personal experiences that are usually derived through trial and error. This is a good thing, most of the time. Sometimes wrong advice may be shared, but mistakes are okay, as long as we learn from them.

In all the research I've done on food plots in blacktail habitats, there have been a handful of helpful resources. Seed companies around the area have helped answer questions, as have some deer-oriented organizations. People who have worked with supplemental feeds also offered guidance. Even the big whitetail food plot experts back east have been of help, along with the internet.

Before planting a plot, it's a good idea to have goals in mind. Ask yourself how much property you want to devote to a plot, if you want to hunt over it in September or November, or if winter and spring is when you want to try and help out the deer. Maybe it's a combination of all of the above.

At one of the many sportshows I attend, I was introduced to Dave Douglas, a man who later answered many of my questions on blacktails and food enhancement. Dave is the owner of Blacktail Specialties, a company that provides quality nutrition for blacktail deer and other species in the Pacific Northwest (www.blacktailspecialties.com).

What impressed me most about Dave's approach was that his finished product didn't look like a well manicured field. In fact, because he blends his plantings with the natural habitat, using natural food, it's tough to even tell there's a "food plot." You won't find Dave putting in acres of picture-perfect fields to hunt over. In fact, he doesn't actually think of his plantings as food plots in the form that they've been recognized in recent years around the hunting community. Dave's philosophy is that the animals should live, eat and drink in the woods.

Dave's objective is to develop highly nutritious protein blends that will get blacktails through the winter and help big bucks maximize their true genetic potential. Dave has a unique background which led to his development of Blacktail Specialties, but it was hunting, and the lack of big racked-bulls in the area that he elk hunted that sparked his interest. Through research he learned that the bulls' racks in the area he hunted never had a chance to reach their full potential due to poor quality food. If this was the case for elk, it could also apply to deer, Dave reasoned.

Dave's dedication has paid off, as he's helped many blacktail hunters implement planting programs that have found success in recent years. Perhaps the most impressive to date, two bucks taken off the same property in Washington's Clark County. Dave's clients seeded an area and after watching two specific bucks over a four year period, finally decided to take them. The bucks netted 202-inches and 203-inches, nontypical. Those are giant blacktails, period, especially for Washington.

In helping people get started with their programs (you won't hear Dave call them food plots), he pours over many photos of the prospective land, and has found that a south facing slope is usually best for planting, overall. Next, he'll conduct soil samples. "We have lots of clay in the soils of the Northwest, and you have to break that down, neutralizing it so things can grow," Dave shares. From there, Dave suggests ways to increase the natural growth of key foods in the existing area, and then he looks at which outside food sources to bring in.

The seed blends Dave uses in his plantings are what naturally occur in the Northwest. The thing I like about Dave's approach is that it's all natural, and the best part, there's no need to pipe in constant water – unless you're in northern California where water can be scarce during prime planting times. Natural rains will normally provide the water that's needed for proper growth.

The size of planting you choose depends on the land. Dave suggests devoting 5% of the property for planting. He urges people not to overdo it when it comes to blacktails. "These deer are so diverse in their feeding, one day you might have 20 deer in your feed, the next day, nothing," he points out. "One day they may be eating blackberries, the next day they may pass right by them. This is why I stay with native plants, as the deer are used to a variety of feed, plus they won't hesitate eating on them right away."

Most of the people Dave deals with simply work up the ground by hand, with a long handled rake. This means there's no need for big tractors or four-wheelers with tiller blades. Many of the plots Dave has helped start have been in hilly, brushy, steep country, where it would have been a hassle to get equipment into. Simply select an area, and then work up about 1/4-inch of soil to get the seeds to take. Broadcast the proper amount of seeds then let a good rain work it into the ground. That's it.

As for the actual seed types, native clover, wheat, oats and barley play a big part in what Dave opts to use. He's also developed a brassica, a cross between a turnip and mustard. He says that if the animals leave the brassica alone, it can grow chest-high. They love eating the leaves of the brassica in summer, then picking off stem regrowth in the fall, and coming back for the root in winter.

In the drier blacktail habitats of southern Oregon and northern California, in addition to a seed mix, Dave will use some fescue (rye grass) as a cover feed. This gives the deer something to feed on year-round, when other foods have been eaten. After broadcasting seeds in these arid zones, water it in if no rain is forecast, then leave it alone. Once it gets six or eight inches tall, knock it in half, as this will cause the roots to spread thicker and it reseeds itself nicely the following year.

Depending on the weather, a springtime planting during March through June is good. The ideal places for spring plantings are on the south facing slopes, which will accommodate warm-season crops. In the fall months, it's good to plant in September through November. Here, Dave points out the effectiveness of planting on north-facing slopes for cool-season crops. A key in all this is taking advantage of the sun's position and offering deer what they need to optimize their health on a year-round basis.

There's more rain in the fall, and this is when Dave suggests planting your first crop. Start with winter wheat, oats and maybe buckwheat, and let it grow all winter. In the spring, till it into the ground to add nutrients. At this point, it's time to start your customized growing program.

One mistake Dave often sees being made is when people are planting on their own; they try and cut corners by purchasing pasture grade feed. This is a B-grade feed which Dave says is designed for hays to grow and be cut for livestock use. The digestive systems of cattle and horses can withstand the woody stems of this feed, and though some deer may eat it, usually they'll just pluck what few leaves are on it, and then move on. "Deer won't spend much time in these fields because they can't utilize the nutrients," concludes Dave. "To maximize deer usage, you'll want to get custom-made, forage grade feed suited for the ground you intend to plant."

Due to the many elements involved in planting proper forage, Black-tail Specialties offers and entire planting program to help people out. Dave has established a longtime relationship with many clients, including hunting organizations, state agencies and timber companies, in an effort to help them turn out nutrient-rich, natural foods deer and other wildlife will benefit from.

Once your crops start to grow, the maintenance end is fairly easy. If it grows too tall, knock it down each spring. This will encourage root dispersion and produce a fuller crop when it reseeds itself. The key to long term success however, is getting the right mixes of plants. In most areas, there's no need for water, just don't do any planting in July and August, as there's not enough rain or moisture in the ground to meet the seed's needs.

When it comes to developing planting programs or all-out food plots, some folks may wish to do it on their own. That's fine, if done correctly. Be sure to prepare your ground properly, get soil tests done so you know the acidity of the ground you're working with, and then get the proper foods to match the environmental conditions and what deer need.

Some folks are having success with clover mixes, soybeans, sweet corn and various legumes. When planting some of these items, it's often necessary to have large areas to devote to it, as the deer can wipe out small sections rather quickly. It's also important to think ahead and plant to provide deer with year-round forage.

As for mineral supplements, there are many different opinions on this and it comes down to the fact blacktails can be finicky. I've heard of guys getting buckets of apples and carrying those into the woods, and having deer devour them. I've heard of guys having deer deplete the apples in their orchards, so they get apples from another area, toss the apples in their orchard and the deer won't touch them. The same is true with minerals. In some areas, blacktails go nuts over them. In other areas, they don't even look at them.

Whether you find salts (not good for deer, so be careful what you get), mineral blocks or minerals in nugget form to attract deer in your areas, one commonality I have heard is that deer love it when these things are worked into the ground. If in a solid form, break up the minerals and disperse on to the ground or atop old stumps or logs. When rain falls, it washes and disperses the nutrients into the ground or woody tissues. The deer will then eat the dirt and other detritus which have absorbed the minerals, just as they do in nature. Once discovered, it's not uncommon for deer to dig several inches into the ground to get the minerals, and they'll usually keep coming back. Mineral supplements can be found at most sporting good stores, gun and bow shops.

We once put out some molasses-based mineral blocks, made by Purina that the blacktails couldn't leave alone. Deer poured out of the woods to grind away on the tasty blocks – it was incredible. I've talked with other hunters, who have tried the same blocks in other areas, and some had the same results, others had deer walk right on by. One thing I've learned in talking with people who experiment with mineral blocks is that in one area deer may love them, in another area, they may not touch them. That's blacktails for you. Keep trying different forms of mineral blocks in the areas you hunt, and find what works. Keep in mind, what works for you might not work for other hunters, and vise-versa.

The more involved you get with plantings and possible

Mineral blocks can be very effective when it comes to keeping blacktail bucks in an area.

food plot development, even minerals, the more you'll discover there's a lot to learn. Even before you get too deeply involved in it all, you'll soon realize there's a lot of science behind it. While planting nutritional feeds may not suit every blacktail hunter's interest, there are some hunters who attest to its effectiveness. That's the beauty of hunting blacktails, each to their own.

Locate Does

As previously mentioned in this chapter, does play a big part in my buck hunting success, and the off season is prime-time for locating and keeping track of does. While does can be found during the months of January through April, I usually let them rest at this time. I may find pockets of does while out hunting for sheds, and when I do I simply note their location and move on.

My favorite time to locate does is from the middle of May through the month of June. This is the time when does are dropping their fawns, and I've found this to be one of the best times to get an accurate idea of just how many does are in an area. To do it I use fawn bleats, and bring the does to me.

I discovered this by accident when on my first turkey hunt in the late 1970s, while still in junior high school. I was using a diaphragm call, and though my sounds were less than ideal, I did manage to call in and take a plump tom. But on those inadvertent high notes I hit, the ones where I was glad no one was around to hear me, I had deer respond by coming on the run.

Then I began making the high-pitch distress sounds on purpose, and it worked. One day that spring turkey season I called in 26 does. I had no idea there were that many deer in that ravine.

Since that time so many springs ago, I've used fawn distress calls to bring in does from California all the way up to Alaska; it's attracted a fair number of curious bucks, too. Though I've found doe calling to be most productive in the spring, it will also work during the summer, fall and early winter months. I've never tried it in January through April, for I want the does to be able to relax during these times which can be hard on their bodies. They don't need more stress.

When setting up to call spring does, I try to situate myself on the edge of a clearing, so I can call across it and pull deer out of the brush,

83

into the clearing. Don't worry, it's not like calling bears or coyotes which may hang up on the brushy fringes. Does usually come running.

Ideally, if I can get in a place where I can see 180° degrees or more around me, that's even better. This allows me to not only see what does respond directly in front of me, but also what does may be low in a draw below me, or up high in the timber above me.

If I can find a mix of habitats and call all of them from one place, at the same time, that not only helps to figure out how many deer there are, but reveals where they are at that time of year. For example, a great place to set up is on a ridge where you're calling across a clearing with a brushy creek below, a mix of hardwoods, brush and timber across, and big timber above. Seeing which habitat the deer come out of can be valuable information, especially when it comes to targeting resident deer, for the bucks won't be far from the food, water and shelter that keep the does there.

To produce the actual sounds of a small fawn in distress, I prefer an open-reed mouth call that's capable of reaching high pitches. I like these easy to use calls because they allow you to articulate your lips, teeth and air flow to produce very accurate sounds. One of the things that will amaze you is how high-pitched the cries are of a newborn fawn, and how often they'll make the sounds when separated from their mom. It's no wonder so many predators – namely coyotes, bears, bobcats and cougars – claim so many fawns this time of year. It's also a good lesson in what sounds you should be making if predator hunting in the spring, especially if looking to help local deer populations.

For the calls, I make a quick series of high-pitched sounds, continuously for 30 to 45 seconds. Then I'll wait and listen. Often times, when does are close they'll come charging in within the first few seconds of calling. I'll wait a minute or so, and then repeat the sounds. If nothing responds within five minutes, 10 minutes max, I'll move on.

Keep in mind, the objective is to get does to reveal themselves. It's different than predator hunting, where you're trying to get sly animals all the way within shooting range. With spring doe calling, you're emitting a distress sound that signals, "Hey, I'm a lost fawn over here, and I'm scared...someone come save me!" Does are very maternally protective this time of year, even if she knows it's not her fawn making the sounds.

Simple, high-pitched whines that sound like, "Eeeeeaaaaahh... eeeeeeaaaaaahh, in short, quivering bursts are what you want. Keep in mind, newborn fawns have small lungs, so don't blow on the calls too aggressively or too loud, the does may not respond.

Numerous times I've had does run up to within 10 yards of me, and have had as many as eight at a time come in. The interesting part here is that many of the does came from a considerable distance, not only from directly across the clearing in front of me, but from the top and bottom of the canyon, too. Also of interest is how close an amped-up doe will come, even after she's made clear eye contact with you.

Not that you're seeking an up-close encounter, but sometimes does respond within five seconds of calling, and won't leave. I think having does milling around the calling sight has helped me pull more does out of the woods, too. It offers security in numbers, and sends the message that "something's up." The more does you can see, the better, as this can be valuable information, no matter where you hunt bucks.

If my target is a late season, migratory buck, then I'll head into the higher foothill regions where I know migratory bucks will be heading late in the fall. I won't mess with hiking into the high country to find does, for they'll also drop in elevation during the migration. For migratory bucks, I'm looking for pockets of resident does on the fringe elevations of where these bucks migrate to. For public land hunters, this is scouting time well spent.

Come hunting season, if I'm going to be targeting resident bucks, I try and find as many pockets of does as possible, then get out of there. I'll make note of where I found the does and why they might be there. Though their spring food sources may change come hunting season, the does will not move far. All I need to know is that there are does in the area, and if there are a lot of them, there's no question bucks will not be far.

In extremely brushy river bottoms where I hunt, where I know bucks are holding year-round and where seasonal food, water and shelter are easy to come by, I'll concentrate on calling the outer fringes, to see where the does come from. The bucks will be there, hiding safely, deeper in the brush.

Bottom line, finding the does in spring increases the likelihood of finding the bucks come fall. As DHLS has progressed, I've found spring scouting for does to be valuable for me, as it allows me to see how many does survived the winter and what condition they're in. There are places I used to hunt that were teaming with does; now they are void due to DHLS. Eventually, healthy does will relocate into these prime habitats, and the bucks will follow. But until that time, it's important that I cover ground, locate new doe populations, and then do my homework to figure out where the bucks will likely be.

Chapter Three
The Early Season
(July - September)

For most early blacktail hunters the actual season doesn't open until early September. But, fortunately, that's not the case for everyone. There are some excellent early season hunts out there, meaning the mid-summer months don't have to be spent just scouting.

In California's A Zone, for instance, the archery season usually opens the second week in July. While most blacktail hunters are still scouting for deer at this time, California provides people the opportunity to get out there and hunt, early. Alaska's Sitka blacktail seasons traditionally open in early August, offering hunters another chance at early season blacktail.

Depending on the year, some early blacktail archery season's open in late August, when the bucks are still in velvet. At the same time, there are some early draw hunts for rifle hunters, one of the best being Oregon's High Cascade blacktail hunt.

In this chapter we'll look at what I call the early season, which takes in the months of July, August and September. I've dubbed these three months the early season because in the respective areas where the first of the year's deer seasons open, it is, indeed, early. Another key point, during these months bucks are behaving differently than any other time.

Even if the state or area you hunt does not have an early season, this is still one of the best times to get out and scout. In fact, many accomplished blacktail hunters regard July and August as the best two months of the year to be out scouting for trophy bucks.

Behavior & Scouting

There are two prime times to be in the field when you can actually lay eyes on trophy blacktail bucks. Many hunters consider the November rut to be the best time to watch big bucks. While this can be true, the fact is, many big bucks are on the move during this time of year, either covering ground in search of does or physically chasing them. Because of this escalated level of movement, you may see a buck one day and he may be gone the next.

While my favorite month to observe buck behavior is in November, during the rut, personally, July and August are my preferred months to locate and learn about big bucks. This is due to the simple reason that during July and August, when the bucks are still in velvet, they are relaxed and carrying out daily routines. They're not wired, letting hormones dictate how they act, running through the woods chasing does.

The best way to learn about a blacktail deer, or any big game animal for that matter, is to observe it, undisturbed. If you can watch a buck without his knowing you are around, it's amazing how much can be learned.

In July and August, blacktail bucks are usually hanging out in small bachelor groups, or alone. One thing I have observed, at least in the areas where I hunt, is that when a bachelor herd of bucks hangs out together, and there's a trophy buck among them, he often lets them make the first move, then follows.

Finding early season bucks by themselves, or in bachelor groups, is a great way to observe their behavior.

On several occasions I've watched smaller forked-horns, three-points and little 4x4s work their way out of bedding areas into feeding zones, only to be followed by a bigger, wiser buck. Virtually every time I've watched this, the smaller bucks go first. Many times the big bucks won't even use the same trail. Often times they'll enter the feeding area uphill from where the smaller bucks are, then eventually work their way down to the rest of the group. Big bucks make very few mistakes.

There are two main reasons July and August are prime months for either locating or killing big bucks. The first has to do with the racks still being in velvet, the second with the bucks' daily routine.

The fact that antlers are still in velvet is perhaps the biggest advantage to the hunter, or scout. Developing velvet racks pump a great deal of blood through their veins, and are very sensitive when touched. For brush-country blacktail hunters, this means the deer can be seen in the open on a regular basis, a rarity when compared to the other months of the year.

In some of the brushy terrain I hunt, the forest fringes are so thick, bucks won't walk through them to reach their usual core bedding area. Instead, they'll bed in meadows, clearcuts or along rock faces. By staying in these open habitats, they don't risk damaging their racks, and they're usually very near a food source, not too far from water.

During July and August, bucks will devote many hours to feeding during the course of a day in an effort to maximize antler growth — their headgear is a major display of dominance, which gains them breeding rights — and amasses body fat for the upcoming rut and winter. Because consuming nutritious food is a key objective of bucks this time of year, spending all day in the field, either scouting or hunting, can be highly beneficial. The hunter's worst enemy this time of year is the heat, so be prepared to handle it. At the same time, when it comes to locating bucks, excessively high temperatures can be a trophy hunter's best friend, for it forces the bucks to find shade.

When searching for early season bucks in velvet, one thing I've learned is how active they are. When I'm scouting in the hot months of July and August, it's not uncommon to see deer up and feeding until 10:00 a.m. At the same time, they may start feeding again in the late afternoon or early evening, well before shade hits the mountainside.

When these bucks bed down, it's amazing to see how little cover it takes to actually hide them. From what I've observed, their number one priority when bedding is staying shaded. This is where the hot temperatures can help hunters. Hot day's mean deer will often bed in places where it's easy for humans to see them, like under trees, at the base of logs or stumps, and against rock outcroppings. It doesn't take much shade to keep a deer happy, so be sure and look over all the potential bedding places, even the obvious ones.

Deer will also spend the day in tall grass, against brush and amid ferns – anywhere they can gain shade. In fact, the small shaded areas are among my favorite to glass, for the simple fact the shade doesn't last long, meaning the deer have to get up and reposition themselves in the shade during the course of the day. I've spotted an incredible number of bucks between the hours of 11:00 a.m. and 3:00 p.m, the hottest part of the day, when they get up to reposition themselves in the shifting shade. Sometimes they'll get up, take a step or two and lay back down in the shade. Sometimes they'll take their time, stretch, and then lay back down. Other times they may get up, take a few bites of food, then move to another spot of shade.

Due to the moving shade, midday is one of my favorite times to glass. I also like blue-sky days over cloudy ones for the simple reason it gives the deer less shade to lay in.

The second reason I like scouting so much in the early season is because this is the only time I've been able to consistently pattern big buck movements. Patterning blacktail bucks comes back to the habitat you hunt them in. How the deer move within one habitat can greatly vary as to how they move in another. Remember the six faces of blacktails outlined earlier in this book? We're back at seeing how different bucks can behave based on where they live.

Radio telemetry and trail camera studies have revealed that once blacktail bucks shed their velvet, rarely will they use the same trail day after day. In fact, big bucks have multiple trails they travel on, which makes patterning them even more of a challenge. This is why getting out in the early season is important, for it's one of the only times you can actually watch big bucks and pattern their movements.

Over the years I've patterned early season blacktails in every habitat I've hunted them in, including Sitka blacktails high in their alpine dwellings. When I go in to an area, there are specific things I look for, the two most important factors of which are food and shade. Find where deer bed in the shade and on what they feed and most of the work is done.

In the valley floor and foothill habitats I hunt, blacktails seek new blackberry growth this time of year. While there are other foods available, this is one they focus on. They'll also be munching on various herbaceous leaves on the fringes of open areas, and grazing on weeds in wide open hillsides.

One July I spent quite a bit of time scouting a specific spot in the foothills of the Cascades. The area had lots of feed, but it was concentrated in a small pocket that was not easy to access, or see. What made it more alluring to the deer was that it was bordered by big timber that was wide-open underneath and had no brush growing along its fringes. This meant the deer had the safety and shelter of the timber to bed in, rather then being stuck in the open.

I'd seen a dandy 4x4 and a few other smaller bucks with him. I watched his rack mature nicely through all of July, August and early September. I wanted my wife to try for this buck in the general rifle season, so I continued looking for him off and on in September. As the early October season drew closer, the big buck went nocturnal, but the other bucks still traveled the same route in the waning hours of light to reach the food source.

Though the four-point never showed, my wife did

Tiffany Haugen scored on this blacktail after it's movements had been patterned. The early season is prime-time for studying blacktail bucks.

91

take a three-point with only a few minutes of daylight remaining. It goes to show how these deer can be patterned, and had I hunted that four-point in the early archery season, I know I could have taken a crack at him from a tree stand.

Due to the abundant food in the valley floors and the deer's small home range here, these are also predictable places to pattern deer in July and August. Some of the toughest places to pattern bucks, at least for me, have been in the Coast Range. I think this is due to the fact so much food exists in the area, and the deep, rugged, shaded canyons offer deer multiple forms of shade.

In the coastal hills, if looking to pattern bucks, spend time searching the edges of open units that are anywhere from one to six years of age. Often times these units offer feed that's more attractive to bucks, so they'll keep coming back to them day after day. Some of the biggest coastal blacktails I've patterned have been on the edges of logged units. But as soon as they shed their velvet, I lost track of them.

When it comes to Cascade, open country and high country blacktails, I think these are the easiest bucks to pattern in July and August. This is so because the terrain they occupy is big and a high percentage of it is open – at least by blacktail standards – while their food and water sources are concentrated. Talk with some successful early season hunters and you'll learn why this is their favorite time to hunt big blacktails, even over the rut.

When scouting or hunting in this big country, look for bucks feeding in open terrain. Sometimes they're in the middle of meadows or logged units. Other times they're right on the fringes. Where you find deer depends on the density of food in the area and how far and through what type of terrain they have to travel through to reach it.

A lack of human pressure is one of the most appealing aspects of early season hunting and scouting. Few people go through the rigors of backcountry blacktail hunting, and fewer spend time scouting this area. At the same time, rifle tags that are allotted in such regions are usually regulated, so hunting pressure is light. The exception lies in some of California's high country, where a massive labyrinth of hiking trails provide easy access for archers. Then again, there are plenty of places to hunt in the A Zone.

In the high, open and Cascade blacktail habitats, search for deer up and feeding well in to late morning. From a distance, watch where they feed, and through a high-powered spotting scope, try to determine what they're feeding on. Observe the deer as they move, and try to determine how they monitor the wind as they mill around. Also, try and narrow down where they might bed. Some will bed in the open, making it easy, others will move into the open timber to bed in heavy shade.

If scouting, don't worry about following bucks to find their exact bedding spot, it's not that important. What you want to look for are places where you can set up along their path of travel come hunting season, and have a good chance of killing a big buck. This is why patterning them is important; to make sure they are using the same trails each day.

If you're hunting, it's a different story. When a buck beds, that's the best time to put the move on him. In higher elevations, make sure the thermals have shifted and that the warmer, less dense air is rising. This means stalking in from above, or at a side-hill angle is best. In rocky terrain where there's a chance of knocking rubble loose and having it roll downhill and potentially spook a deer, try coming in more from the side, hopefully from behind the deer, yet still from above it. Whatever angle you come in from, keep checking the wind at all times. We'll focus more on early season hunting tactics later in this chapter.

No matter which form of Columbia blacktail you hunt, when or where, early season scouting can be one of the most valuable times to learn what's really out there. Being able to actually lay eyes on trophy bucks, and see the number and caliber of bucks in an area can give you an optimistic outlook you never thought possible in the world of blacktail hunting.

A young hunter I talked with one day, summed it up best when he discovered just how helpful July and August scouting missions could be. This guy was a general season rifle hunter who has killed many fine blacktails on public land, including some impressive record book bucks. His scouting trips are carried out on mountain bike, into the upper foothills of the Cascade Range. After his first year of scouting he had no idea there were so many bucks out there, and big bucks. Seeing the bucks in velvet confirmed that he'd been hunting in the right places. The bucks are out there, people just have to work hard to find them.

Once a buck sheds the velvet from his rack, usually by the first few days in September, his behaviors start to change. Interestingly, in the areas I've scouted, it seems that once a buck starts shedding his velvet, all the bucks in that area are done with the process within two or three days of one another. Big bucks seem to shed their velvet first, while some younger bucks may keep it a week or two longer. With the antler growing finished, a buck doesn't have the sensitive growing velvet on his rack to protect it. This means he can return to the thicker bedding places in his core area. It also means he'll start feeding at night, in the safety of darkness.

Two days prior to shedding his velvet, this buck was caught on film in broad daylight. Once he stripped the velvet, he went nocturnal.

There's also a slight hormonal shift that takes place within bucks at this time. Now begins the period of pre-rut, and the big boys take notice of what deer, bucks and does, are in their area. The bucks, especially the younger age class, will also start sparring with one another in an effort to see who might be the best on the block.

If you hold an early season tag, September can be one of the best times to fill it on a big buck as their movements are not yet hindered by human activity. This lack of intrusion is an important factor that separates the early season from the mid-season. In the mid-season, it only takes one day of increased human activity to greatly alter the movement of trophy bucks.

No matter what your objective, to find a buck or kill it, there's no time like the early season to get it done. Conditions are tough, no doubt, but when it comes to physically seeing bucks, you'll be hard-pressed to find a better time than the early season. Even if your hunts don't open until October or November, making an effort to get out there in the early season, to see what deer are around, can pay dividends. If nothing else, it will give you confidence just knowing big bucks are out there, and in the world of trophy blacktail hunting, confidence means everything.

Trail Cameras

When it comes to modern technologies, in my opinion, nothing has impacted the world of blacktail deer hunting more than trail cameras. Throughout blacktail hunting history, the biggest challenge has been to know what's out there. Trail cameras are now revealing answers.

Each state wildlife agency tries to conduct census counts in an effort to learn blacktail populations, but even that's tough. Like being a weatherman trying to predict a week-long forecast, it's near impossible to know just how many blacktails are out there.

In the past, wildlife findings combined with hunter success reports have worked to answer some questions. But now, hunters are able to place cameras in the woods and see for themselves how many deer are out there. For a handful of hunters, catching glimpses of just how big some of these bucks are is all that really matters.

When it comes to setting up a camera, look for trails on which deer movement is concentrated. Main trails are good at providing information on overall deer numbers, but taking in to consideration that mature blacktail bucks rarely travel along primary trails, and don't often use the same trail on consecutive days, you'll need to find secondary routes to learn about the big boys. This is why it's a good idea to invest in multiple cameras, so they can be set on various trails.

When situating the camera itself, do so in a manner that catches deer quartering toward or away from the lens. Avoid rigging the camera

**More hunters are turning to trail cameras to help
learn about blacktails in their hunting areas.**

where it shoots at a 90° angle to the trail as this will not only result in potentially spooking nervous bucks, but also in catching only a glimpse of their bodies as they move through. Set up the camera so you can capture multiple images of a deer's profile as it approaches or walks away.

For clear, crisp shots, position the camera so it's no more than 20 feet from where you expect the photo to be snapped – this is especially true if using cameras with night vision. Hang the camera about waist to chest high, as this will eliminate most small critters from being photographed and will capture full-body images of deer. Be careful not to position cameras so they shoot into direct sunlight, as the images will not turn out.

Once you've captured some images, study them. You can download photos on the computer and enlarge them to see just how big that buck really is. You can also learn a lot about a deer's movements. If, for example, the deer is walking downhill past the camera in the evening, it's likely going to feed. If the deer is walking uphill, past the camera in

**Blacktail deer can be found from ocean beaches
to the tops of the Cascade Range.**

For the author, his introduction to blacktail hunting began at an early age. Here he is at age two with his grandpa Lupon, who passed away two years later while in the blacktail woods.

Haugen (left) rattled in his first blacktail in 1979. This buck was taken by his boyhood friend, Andy Bruin.

Haugen grew up hunting blacktails in the foothills of Oregon's Cascade Range. This is one of his most memorable bucks.

Noted author and blacktail fanatic, Bob Robb, arrowed this Boone & Crockett class buck during an early archery season.

DAN GIBSON PHOTO

One of the greatest challenges in field judging blacktails
lies in being able to get a long enough look at them.
This one posed perfectly.

STEVE LEE PHOTO

Finding monster bucks like this is what early season
scouting is all about.

Haugen's best Sitka blacktail came from Kodiak Island.
This record book buck came running in to
a rattle bag during a snow storm.

Cougar kills can disrupt the behavior of even the
most sedentary blacktails.

Parrey Cremeans made a perfect stalk on this 198 7/8"
California inland blacktail.

This photo re-creation shows what Cremeans saw
before pulling the trigger on his monster buck.

Joe Schmit took this mid-150", heavy-racked buck,
from Oregon's Cascades.

These foothill deer taken by the author's family, came from the same area, within view of the city of Springfield, OR. The top buck sported a 27 ½" spread. These are pure blacktails.

A young Scott Haugen with a blacktail taken during his high school years. After shooting this deer, a giant buck stepped out of the brush. Today, Haugen continues to learn from these elusive bucks.

Pounding a club on the ground brought this buck in on the run. No rattling or calling was required.

Parrey Cremeans arrowed this dandy buck in California's
early season.

The author's father, Jerry
Haugen, sat on a trail and
shot this stout-racked
buck at close range with
a muzzleloader.

One of the author's greatest blacktail moments was taking his then four year old son, Braxton, on the blood trail of this buck. This is where, and how, future blacktail hunters are shaped.

Haugen spot-and-stalked his way to this impressive 6x6 while hunting the floor of Oregon's Willamette Valley.

The author took this Boone & Crockett class buck from
a ground blind during Oregon's late archery season.

After 17 days of hunting, both Scott and Tiffany
connected on their bucks, and their sons were there
to experience it. It's family moments like this that
build generations of blacktail hunters.

the morning, it's likely going to bed. Knowing this will help you decide where to place stands, or yourself, so you can intercept the buck come time to hunt.

Where you actually choose to set your trail camera depends on the time of year. In the early season, hit trails connecting known areas of feed. Sometimes in the throat of funnels and along benches where trails exist can be good early season settings. Trails that skirt the edges of clearings and patches of brush the deer feed on are also good. If you have a food plot or planting program in place, now is the time to see the caliber of bucks using it.

Believe it or not, setting trail cameras in the high, open country can also pay off this time of year, even if you don't intend on hunting those deer until late in the year, once both the rut and migration have kicked-in. Here is a case in point.

Good friend and blacktail nut, Jeremy Toman, and one of his buddies set up trail cameras in July. They were at 3,000 feet in elevation, in Oregon's Cascades, obviously on public land. Their objective was to capture bucks on film now, in the middle of summer, then go in during the November archery season and try to get them prior to any migration that might occur. Their plan worked, and they learned something valuable along the way.

During July, Toman caught many deer on film, and a couple of exceptional bucks. One was a beautiful, clean 4x4, the other a massive-racked brute with all sorts of junk on his bases. Due to commitments, the duo couldn't make it in to their hunting area until the first of December. After a long hike, the hunters questioned their sanity, given the more than a foot of snow they had to push through.

When they got to the area where their trail cameras had spent the summer, fresh tracks and rubs were thick. Toman set up, rattled and called, and within minutes the big, nontypical buck came running in. Toman arrowed the buck 25 yards from where he'd snapped his photo with the trail camera five months prior. It scored over 150 Boone & Crockett inches. A few sets later, the other 4x4 came in, and Toman's buddy made a perfect shot on that, a buck that scored in the mid 120s.

Even in the Cascade Range, trail cameras have value. Michael Parks caught this buck on film four months earlier, then took him during late bow season.

This is one example of how valuable trail cameras can be if you're willing to put in the time and effort to scout, even in the high country. Toman was pleased with the results, and learned a valuable lesson that just because there was more than a foot of snow on the ground, the deer hadn't left the area. Blacktails are tough creatures and if the feed is good and the does are sticking to an area, the bucks won't be far. Oh yeah, he also discovered how priceless trail cameras can be for discovering big bucks, for without them, he wouldn't have had any idea the two bucks they killed were even around.

For the early season blacktail hunter, trail cameras are very effective for locating resident bucks you know will be in the area come hunting season. This is true no matter where you hunt. I know of several hunters, myself included, who have benefited from what early season trail camera setups have revealed. In many cases, these camera's showed bucks we had no idea were in the area. At the same time, they captured bucks we knew were there, and upon closer inspection of the photos, allowed us to more accurately rough-score their racks to decide if they were deer we wanted to hunt.

When it comes to early season camera placement, if there's an area where you can work minerals into the earth and get the deer to start coming in, you'll be in good shape. Once they start visiting the site, put up your trail camera. Because the hot, dry, late summer months see a drop in food quality in many blacktail habitats, these supplements can help the deer, and the concentrated feeding area it provides creates a great opportunity to photograph blacktails in high numbers.

Though trail cameras are a great tool to be used on a year-round basis, you'd be hard-pressed to find a time when they are more valuable than in the early season. What I like about these devices is that they keep you thinking in an effort to learn more about these elusive deer. One thing I have learned through my use of trail cameras is that we don't know nearly as much as we think we do about these deer. And with so much yet to be learned, we – at least I – can use all the help that's available.

Hunting Tactics

As with other times of the year, early season hunting tactics are habitat, weather and behaviorally dependent. The approaches which can be applied come down to how effectively you can get yourself into shooting range without being busted, which can be a major challenge this time of year. Often temperatures break the century mark in the early season, and the ground is so dry and noisy it can make taking a simple step nearly impossible without alerting animals.

On top of the challenging conditions surrounding the early season, the behavior of the animals play a large part in how we try to get them. This time of year deer may bed for ten hours a day, versus being active most of the day come November. They will lie in different areas, move differently and interact with one another differently than later in the year.

The early season can be the most challenging time to hunt cagey blacktails. Then again, if you go about it properly, it can be the most productive time of year to hunt them. The number of big bucks which can be seen in the early season can boggle the mind. And the number of stalks and close-encounters, even shot opportunities, can be nothing short of spectacular. In this section, we'll take a close look at the top three early season hunting strategies and how to best apply them.

Keep in mind that the strategies to be outlined are based on habitat, current conditions and how deer are behaving within their varied habitats this time of year. It doesn't matter what tag you have or which weapon you're hunting with, the objective is to get close, within your effective shooting range.

Spot & Stalk

Spot and stalk is the most common approach when talking blacktail deer hunting strategies. No matter what time of the season a hunter finds himself afield, or if they're hunting with bow, rifle, muzzleloader or shotgun, locating a deer then walking it up, is what most blacktail hunters prefer to do, and tend to have the most success doing.

In my line of work, one thing I always love sharing with whitetail hunters from back east is the thrill of spot and stalk hunting blacktails. If you want to find out how good your hunting skills are, hit the ground with a pack on your back, binos' around your neck, weapon in hand and go stalk to within shooting range of a trophy class buck. Not only is this the most challenging form of hunting, but it's the most rewarding, no matter what time of year it's applied. It also requires a great deal of patience, knowledge and skill to become proficient.

Given the tough conditions, early season spot and stalk hunting is the most challenging of all. Here, locating a buck is the easy part, and really, that can seem near impossible at times. Closing to within shooting range is the hardest part.

The first part of the equation, the spot, is the easier of the two steps, but there are important things to know which can help increase your ability to find deer. No matter where an early season hunt finds me – on a river bottom, high in the mountains, in open terrain or along brush-choked, timbered ridgelines – I always have quality optics. The quality of glass being used in today's crafting of optics is unparalleled, and the number of good manufacturers keeps growing. So what works best? That's a personal call, and the general rule of thumb, which is a good one, is to invest in the most expensive glass you can afford. In other words, when it comes to optics, be it binoculars, spotting scopes, rangefinders and/or gun scopes, the more you spend, the higher the quality will be. I have the luxury of testing out numerous makes and models of optics every year, and my conclusion is always the same...the more expensive, the higher the overall quality, period.

On an early season hunt I'll have my 10x42 binoculars, a rangefinder and spotting scope. Which spotting scope I use depends on the terrain I'm hunting in. If I'm hiking long distances, I want something light and compact. If I'm glassing from roads, I'll go with something heavier and of higher magnification. As for binoculars, I like the 10x42s over the 8x42 for the extra magnification they offer. As for rangefinders, I prefer models with built-in inclinometers for those steep angle shots which are common this time of year.

When glassing, there is a specific approach I follow, which maximizes my time afield. Keeping in mind that in the summer months, early mornings are cool and the air is dense, so wind currents are moving downhill. This also means that since the wind is moving downhill, I want to be either below or across from deer, not directly above them. If I can glass from above, across canyons where I know deer won't smell me, I'll do it as this puts me in good stalking position for later in the day.

When I search for deer, I get comfortable and start systematically breaking down the country as I look through my binoculars. I'll scour the most obvious places first, in hopes of finding bucks either feeding or moving towards a bedding area. Usually a buck's bedding area will be on higher ground than where he feeds, which is another reason not to position yourself directly above a buck to start off the morning.

I'll continue dissecting the land, glassing specific portions of ground. If I don't spot anything, I'll look over the ground several times, especially if I know there are good bucks in the area. It doesn't take much cover to hide a deer, and I want to make sure I don't miss a thing. If I see nothing with binoculars, I'll often switch to a spotting scope and search for parts of a deer.

When searching, look for parts of deer, not necessarily the whole body. Look for ears twitching, the tines of a rack, the horizontal outline of a belly in the brush, a rump patch and so on. Rarely do I ever spot a deer presenting its whole body. Speaking of body, since a blacktail's summer coat is so red this time of year, look for those patches of color as well. The early season is the easiest time to visually locate a buck, no question.

Gaining the high ground, then using a spotting scope to study bucks, is a smart way to hunt trophy blacktails.

Once a buck is located through binoculars, I switch to the spotting scope to evaluate the size of its rack. Though spotting scopes can be cumbersome to carry around, they are worth every bit of effort. The amount of legwork they can save is invaluable. Rather than spotting a buck then walking a great distance to glass again in order to see how big he really is, simply set up the spotting scope. Not only can a spotting scope save you hours of walking during the course of a hunt, it will increase your hunting time. Spotting scopes are not an option; they're a necessity on most of my early season hunts.

When I find a buck I know I want to try and shoot, I'll observe him for as long as I can to figure out a game plan for phase two of this approach, the stalk. If it's an early morning spot, then I'll watch how and where the deer moves, especially how he uses the wind. Though I may not be able to get on that buck on the first day, I can learn a lot by watching him, whereby figuring out where I need to be the following day in order to get a shot.

As bucks move, watch how they use their sense of smell and the wind. One thing I've observed over the years is that deer let the wind decide where they will feed, and sometimes move. They will often move with the wind when going to feed. Think about it, that's with the wind, not against it. Deer moving from their bedding area in the evening usually travel downhill, with the falling wind, to reach feed. In the morning, as the air heats up and starts rising up the hills, the deer will eventually be moving with it as morning progresses. This is one reason early season hunts can be so effective, because the wind patterns are fairly consistent and predictable. The key is to know how the deer use them.

Earlier I mentioned that I don't like being directly above a buck early in the morning, and that's true. When the air is moving downhill, a deer will smell you. But the minute those thermal currents heat up, become less dense and start moving uphill, then I want to be above the deer. As a deer moves with the wind, they can keep an eye out for predators in front of them, and smell them coming from behind. Since we, as hunters, are predators, we have to outsmart the deer, and this means using the wind to our advantage in this game of spot and stalk.

If I locate a buck and don't have a chance of getting in front of him, or closing the deal due to uncertain shifts in air currents, I'll wait and watch, and if I can follow him to where he beds down, great. At this point I'll look to see if he beds in the sun or in the shade. Usually the first bed of the day is in the sunlight in an attempt warm up. If they bed in the sun, I wait.

There's no telling how long a deer will stay bedded in direct sunlight. But one thing is for certain, they will move. I've watched them bed for less than 15 minutes before moving to shade. Other times they've spent over two hours soaking up the sun. To try and move within shooting range while a buck is bedded in the sun, especially in archery season, is usually a low percentage proposition.

Now, if the buck beds in heavy shade right away, chances are he'll stay there for a while, especially if the wind is consistently moving uphill. Likewise, once a buck initially beds in the sun, then moves to shade, chances are he'll stay there a while. When a buck I want hits the shade, I start studying the land for an approach angle.

If I can see the buck, that's ideal, for it allows me to carefully survey the surrounding landscape through the spotting scope and determine if I can get within shooting range. If I can't see where he beds, especially if he moved into the trees, then I'll approach very slowly from above and at an angle, making sure to use the wind while looking for body parts of a bedded deer. More times than not, a buck will bed with a log, rock, tree, tall grass or some sort of object at his back. This means I often look for a place where I can get within shooting range, and sit, waiting for the buck to stand for a shot.

It's nerve-racking, because in these situations where you're forced to wait for a buck to stand to present a shot, all the year's hard work comes down to this one moment in time. Sometimes you'll wait minutes, sometimes hours before getting a crack. It's the ultimate test of skill, nerves and patience.

One stalk I had on a record book 4x5 couldn't have been more perfect. I watched a bachelor herd of seven bucks move uphill from their nightly feeding area, then lay down in the sun. It was early September and it was going to be a hot day. Two hours later the bucks all got up and starting walking higher up the hill, toward shade.

They all bedded down in the same little bowl, looking different directions. There was no hope of my getting within bow range. Then my target deer stood, stretched, moved about 40 yards above the rest of the deer and laid back down in the shade. Giving the wind an hour to stabilize, I was finally able to make my move.

Given where he was bedded, I came in from above and to the side. I slipped off my shoes, put on another pair of thick wool socks, and tiptoed to within 15 yards of that buck. It took me over an hour to close the last 50 yards, but I got to where I wanted to be. Unfortunately, I didn't have a shot.

There I sat, arrow knocked, release in my loop, trying to remain calm until the buck stood. Seconds turned to minutes, minutes to more than an hour. Then things went from good to bad, fast.

Two of the bucks that were bedded below decided to join the big boy. Though they locked on to me at 30 yards, they didn't smell me. For several minutes I was pinned down, daring to not even blink. As the two bucks drew closer, they grew more curious. Then one blew through his nose. Immediately I came to full-draw and looked down at my buck, which jumped to his feet and lunged forward.

The buck moved far enough forward that some brush covered his vitals. Still, I thought I could thread an arrow through there for a high lung shot. The arrow glanced off the brush and sailed right over his back; a clean miss. Everything came together in one tense, fury-filled moment, when a million decisions had to be made in a split second. Truth is, I should have made the shot, but blew it. I was simply too jacked-up. The day I lose that adrenaline rush come crunch time, is the day I give up hunting.

When I spot a deer in a stalkable position, I assess the wind and the terrain directly above and to both sides of him. This will provide multiple pieces of information to utilize when the stalk commences. One thing to keep in mind, the closer you get to the area through which you planned your stalk, the more things look different. Actually walking through the country you glassed from a mile or more away may have you guessing as to whether or not you're even on the right ridge.

In addition to the wind and the terrain, I mark key points of land. Look for big rocks, tall trees, snags, unique openings, different colored grass and more. Not only can these landmarks provide needed cover during your stalk, but they reassure you that you're on the right path to your buck.

Depending on how strong the wind, my last 50 to 100 yards is usually spent stalking in sock feet during the early season. The conditions are so dry, boots or shoes are almost a certain give away. I'll carry an extra set of heavy wool socks and when it's time, will slip off my boots and drop my pack, then put on the second layer of socks. Not only do these socks make for quiet walking, they also allow you to feel branches, rocks and twigs that might make noise should you step heavy on them. They also cushion pain when landing on sharp, potentially noisy objects. When you feel such things, don't apply pressure. Instead, lift your foot then carefully reposition it for the next step.

If you don't like the idea of leaving your boots and pack behind – you may want to mark them with orange ribbon, so they'll be easier to find – there is another option. There are many forms of boot covers on today's market. These are fleece-type booties that slip over the outside of your boots and make for quiet walking. They're not as quiet as sock feet, but they are far more silent then boot soles. I've stalked to within bow range of many animals with these booties, and they do work.

Another tool I rely heavily on during a stalk is a windcheck bottle. I prefer a squeeze bottle that shoots a long stream of white powder into the air. I like the stream versus a few flakes because I want the windcheck material to travel away from my body and any cover I may be near. This is because the wind currents can be far different a few feet away than what they seem to be on your body. I'll go through several bottles of this stuff during the course of the season.

With the right tools, knowledge and patience, early season spot and stalk hunting can be the most rewarding, and sometimes the most productive approach of all. You'll find that knowing what to do, and when to do it, becomes the most important part of the equation. The more time you can spend in the woods, learning, the more proficient you'll become at spot and stalk hunting.

Tree Stands

Another common approach to getting on early season blacktails is the use of tree stands. Tree stands are a tool we're seeing more and more of in the blacktail woods. Used for years by late season hunters searching for rut-crazed bucks, tree stands are now finding their place in the early season.

To fully understand why tree stands can be so effective, it's important to look at how a deer sees. A deer's pupils are not rounded like a human's, rather are horizontal slits. Combine this with the configuration of rods and cones (more on these in chapter 5), and a deer's vision is quite different from ours. Deer have a very wide field of view, and their eyes are tuned to picking up movement at a distance. Interestingly, the horizontal pupil orients the eyeball to detect movement on or just below the horizon, where predators are active.

Because of their eyeball structure, deer are less adept at detecting movement above the horizon line. When deer stand underneath a tree stand, their ability to look up high and detect movement is even less. While this is no excuse for hunters to get careless and move around, it does explain why we don't get busted as frequently when hunting from stands, versus being on the ground. It also reveals why tree stand hunting can be so effective.

A good friend and one of the most accomplished blacktail hunters I know, Johnny Costello, loves hunting from early season tree stands. Johnny has taken some monster blacktails in the velvet – as well as during other parts of archery season – and his approach to the utilization of tree stands is what makes him such an accomplished hunter. The same holds true of other hunters who have proven their worth by taking big bucks.

Tree stands reveal their true merit in the early season because they allow you to quietly sit smack in a deer's territory without being seen. At least that's the plan. So, where will tree stands work? Just about anywhere blacktails are found this time of year. The question is, "how far do you want to pack them in to your hunting area?"

Previously, we touched on how the early season is the best time to pattern big bucks. Once you've figured out when and where a buck travels, the next step is positioning yourself to kill him. For bowhunters, the closer you get, the better the chance of success.

In situations where spot and stalk simply won't work and you don't want to risk blowing a buck out of the area whereby altering his daily routine, then tree stands may be the best alternative. There are two important aspects surrounding tree stand hunting, and those are hanging the stand in the appropriate place and being able to access it without being seen or smelled.

**Hanging tree stands in the right place is critical.
This early season stand was situated over a water hole,
and the author saw some good bucks from it.**

The placement part comes down to homework. Have you done the homework to figure out which trails bucks are moving on, and figured out where their bedding and feeding areas are? If you've done that, the next step is to figure out a place to hang a stand where you can intercept the deer as they move.

When hunting trails, one thing to keep in mind is what time of day the deer will be passing by the stand. I know of guys who hunt religiously from tree stands in the early season, and their approach is to go high early and low late. In other words, they'll hang at least two stands, and the one they hunt from early in the morning is the one highest on the hill. In contrast, the one they hunt from in the afternoon is the stand that's hung at a lower elevation.

Hunting from a high elevation stand in the morning means you're hoping to catch the buck as he passes by on his way to the bedding area. This may not be a stand you'd want to hunt late in the day for fear of alerting a deer to your presence before he even leaves his bed. Instead, get into the stand well before daylight, allow things to settle down and wait. Hopefully, by the time the buck makes it up to your position the thermals have shifted and are moving uphill with the deer.

When hunting from an evening stand hung along trails at lower elevations, you're hoping to intercept bucks as they enter the feeding area. By early evening the thermals have likely shifted, moving downhill with the buck. This is the ideal situation for the tree stand hunter to be in. If during the night, deer are feeding well into the open, away from where your stand is hung, then this could be an effective spot for a morning hunt. But remember, big bucks usually move for cover well ahead of other deer.

Because wind directions can change, and bucks can utilize different trails to get from point A to point B, hanging multiple stands is a good idea. This keeps you from being limited to one specific stand and forced to hunt from it when the conditions aren't right.

Before entering a stand, check the wind, note the time of day and be cognizant of where the deer should be and in which direction they should soon be heading. At this point you've done the homework. You know what deer are in the area, where they feed, sleep and travel. You've also hung stands in the best places to intercept moving deer. Now, before hiking into a stand, double-check to make sure all the details are in order.

One thing I'll never give away is my wind. Often times I don't care if a deer sees or hears me, but if a big buck smells me, the gig is up, always. This is where scent blocking agents come into play. I've experimented with several, from all-out suits to deodorant, soap, mouthwash and more. All I can say is, if using these products gives you an added sense of security, that little boost of confidence, by all means, use them.

Personally, when preparing to enter into a stand I'll spray down my boots, hands and head, since these are the sources of most foul odors. I'll also spray down my clothes one time. The purpose of this is to try and knock down my scent as I work towards the stand. Sometimes I'll shower with special soaps and apply non-scented deodorants. I don't wash and store my clothes in any special air-tight boxes and I don't use clothes with built-in scent blocking agents. I use the little items that give me a bit of confidence, and no matter what, don't give away the wind.

I've read reports that a deer's nose is anywhere from 300 to 1,000 times better than a dogs. I don't know what the true numbers are and I don't really care. All I need to know is that their noses are far superior to anything humans could ever imagine. In fact, if our noses were as sensitive as a deer's, I guarantee we would not enjoy life thanks to all the horrid odors we'd be exposed to all day, every day.

I've observed thousands of deer over the years and have seen them use their noses with unbelievable acuity. It's the number one sense they depend on for survival, so my mindset is to never be careless and let my wind drift towards an animal. I've tried getting by with it too many times, and it's never worked. Trust me on this one.

Tree stands are a huge advantage because of the simple fact they get your scent off the ground. For blacktails, I like being between 15- to 25-feet in the air. I hedge toward the higher of those two numbers for one reason: air currents. Wind, like water, moves in layers and the higher the layer you can get your scent into, the less likely a deer is to detect it. I have had the wind shift while in a stand, and elected to stay in that stand. I've also had plenty of deer move beneath me, into the wind, but they couldn't smell me because my scent was drifting over them, being carried by the layer of air my stand was in.

Another thing I like about hunting from tree stands is that they allow you to be a passive observer of nature from an aerial position.

From birds to coyotes, does to elk, if you're in a tree stand and none of the critters know it, they'll carry on with life as normal. I think this is important, for the normal activity of these small animals – what I like to call confidence decoys – sends the message to other animals in the woods that all is safe. Make a wrong move with a Steller's jay nearby, and get him squawking uncontrollably, and you'll see what I mean. It's an alert sound all animals in the forest recognize and react to. This is a good example of how important it is to sit still at all times when in the stand, bow or gun at the ready.

Another place early season tree stands have value is near watering holes. Personally, there aren't many areas I hunt where I've been able to pattern the deer as they go to water. I spend lots of time hunting brushy country, where creeks and springs are tough to even see, though you know they are there. And some blacktails get most of the water they need from their food sources. But there are exceptions.

During those hot, early season hunts, targeting waterholes can be very effective. This is especially true in the drier blacktail habitats of California and parts of southern Oregon. July is a good time to scout these water sources and identify which deer are coming to them. If not hunting until August or early September, keep checking the waterholes to see which deer consistently use them. If any heavy, early rains come, be sure to monitor water sources for activity to make sure it doesn't dwindle.

Most of the time when hunting waterholes, simply hang your stand in the tree which offers the best shot angle. Blacktail waterholes are often compact in size and can be surrounded by trees, or have only one growing nearby. Usually, wind direction is not a factor in stand location, since the water sources themselves are so small.

As for the best times to hang tree stands, a general rule is the earlier the better. For my early season bowhunts which normally start around September 1st, I'll start hanging stands in July and early August. Sometimes I'll delay hanging stands to see if the big bucks change their routines once they shed their velvet. When I do decide when and where to place a stand, if possible, I try and hang it during the time of day when the deer will be farthest from the commotion.

When hunting waterholes, stands can stay up year-round, but when hunting trails, stand locations may change from season to season. Then again, if you find a good trail bucks love, you may be shooting deer from the same tree year after year.

One thing I will encourage, and that's to be familiar with your stand, especially if you've never before hunted from one. In selecting a stand, look for what best serves your needs. If you don't like the idea of trimming limbs, installing steps and hopping in a self-climber and shimmying up a tree, then maybe ladder stands are more to your liking. If planning on hiking into the hills a mile or two to hang your stand, then you'll want something lightweight and compact. If you're a rifle hunter, take my word for it, you'll want a stand with a padded railing on it, not only to rest your gun but to lace with camouflage in order to conceal movement.

Before placing a stand in your hunting area, practice with it first. Set it up in a tree, away from your hunting area and make sure you're comfortable with its parameters. Make sure you can move freely while standing and sitting in the stand. Learn your range of motion, and know what shooting angles you like best. This will allow you to know the exact position you want your stand facing when you do secure it in a tree.

For archers, make the time to practice shooting from your stand. Be sure you know the angles at which you can reach full-draw then move and shoot without hitting a cam or limb on any part of the stand. Other than scent, nothing can spook a deer faster than that metal on metal sound. I've learned this the hard way, too.

Also, make sure you practice shooting those sharp, downhill angles. I'd suggest doing this on a life size, 3D deer target, so you can get the angle right with the anatomy of the deer. Be certain you know your effective shooting range from a tree stand, too, as this may be different from standing on solid ground. Now is also the time to practice with that rangefinder featuring a built-in inclinometer. When it comes to bowhunting, there's no such thing as too much practice, especially when tree stands are involved.

Once your stands are set up, survey the trails, waterhole fringes or zones being targeted and trim away what tree limbs are in the way. Do this from both a sitting and standing position. Make sure to cut just enough foliage to allow for comfortable shooting positions to be attained, but don't remove so much so as to expose yourself. Deer will, and do, look up.

Ground Blinds

If hanging from trees makes you nervous, yet you still want to hunt trails or waterholes, ground blinds offer the next best bet. The only downfall about hunting from blinds in the early season is that they can get very hot inside. I once sat in a blind as the outside temperatures shot up to 104°. This made the temperature inside the blind something like 730° – it was hot! If you want to feel what an ear of corn goes through when being steamed, devote yourself to sitting all day in a blind with black interior and no breeze blowing with temperatures near 100°. If nothing else it builds character. During one three day stretch I lost 11 pounds while sitting in a hot blind, despite all the water I was chugging down.

In the right situation, ground blinds are very effective tools for hunting blacktails. The author took one of his better bucks from this setup.

As with tree stands, figuring out where to place your blind is important, and doing the same homework applies. Blinds are excellent for hunting over waterholes, as your focal point is one specific place, the water. Trails can be a bit trickier.

For trail situations, I like blinds that offer a wide field of view. This allows me to see up and down the trail. Many times blacktails start traveling up one trail, and then hop to another, making the more ground you can see, the better. Keep in mind, you won't see near the amount of land from the ground that you will from the trees, so maximizing your field of view is important.

Wherever you pick a spot to hang a tree stand, that area would be good for blind placement, too, for the same reasons. When hunting from ground blinds, I like brushing in all the edges in order to break-up its outline. This includes the front, side and back edges all along the bottom. It's as important to break up the bottom outline as it is the top and sidewall outlines of a blind.

Ideally, if I can place a blind in a slight depression, I've found the animals to be less spooky upon approach. I think this is because the blind blends in better with the surroundings, making it tougher for the deer to see. My least effective blind placements have been on a hill, where deer approach from below and see the blind silhouetted against the sky line.

The biggest benefit of a blind is that it conceals human movement. One of the hardest things for hunters to do is sit still, especially blacktail hunters who've been actively stalking through the woods their whole life. But this doesn't mean you have the green light to fidget about as you wish. In fact, you still need to keep movement to a minimum. And when you move, do it slowly, so as not to draw attention to the blind with the flick of your hand, movement of your head or so on.

To pass the time in a blind, even a tree stand, some people read. I can't do this for two reasons. First, I hate missing anything that goes on in front of me, and two, I'd fall asleep. When spending time in a blind, I take in all the water I can carry and some sunflower seeds. And I don't take my eyes off the land in front of me.

As with tree stands, if you've not hunted from a ground blind, practice shooting from them before heading into the field. One of the first things you'll notice from inside a blind is how far away objects appear to be. Take a rangefinder and use it. Also, for bowhunters, practice shooting from various positions – sitting, kneeling, crouching, sitting back on your feet, one leg up, in a chair, and anything else you can come up with. It's important to learn what you can do in a blind when at full-draw, and this is best accomplished through practice.

One thing I do like about blinds is their versatility. Blinds are easy to set up and take down. The middle and latter parts of the early season are when a buck's habits can literally change overnight, and moving a blind may be necessary to get yourself back into the game.

Ideally it's a good idea to have a blind in place a couple weeks prior to hunting from them, so the deer have a chance to get used to them. This is especially true if having to place the blind on high or level ground, where deer might be nervous the first few times they lay eyes on them. Sometimes I've had no choice but to relocate a blind during the middle of a hunt, and have had bucks walk by them that same day. It's hunting; the animals don't always act the same in every situation.

The beauty of these early season hunting approaches – spot and stalk, tree stands and ground blinds – is that they have applications to everyone, no matter what tool is being used to hunt with, or in which of the varied blacktail habitats you'll be hunting in. Lay the ground work. Study the country and the deer; devise a plan, and a backup plan, to do what's necessary to close the deal. What you just might discover is how enjoyable these early season hunts can be, and how much you can learn from having the opportunity to observe so many deer.

Calling Options

Calling deer is something that's commonly associated with the rut, but as expressed in the previous chapter, I've had good success in the spring, too. In fact, the same principles which apply in the spring also work to attract deer in the early season.

Several blacktail hunters I know have been using fawn distress calls to bring in deer for many years amid the brushy habitat of coastal California. Though does are the ones that predominantly respond to fawn distress calls this time of year, bucks will come to explore out of curiosity.

The sounds you're trying to imitate are those of a fawn in distress. These are high-pitched whines that sound like Eeeeeaaaaahh... eeeeeeaaaaaahh. As the months of August and September pass, fawns mature and in doing so, their lungs more fully develop. This means the distress sounds they make are considerably louder than in the spring. They're also more intense, for at this stage in their life when they let out a cry, it's usually because they are in the jaws of a predator.

114

Personally, the best calling results I've had this time of year when it comes to attracting bucks have been in areas where resident deer are found. I think this is due to the level of curiosity blacktails exhibit and also the dynamics of what's going on within the population at this time.

Blacktails are curious animals, and calling them can be very effective.

Blacktails, even bucks, are very curious animals. I believe part of this has to do with the thick habitat they live in, for when they hear something out of the ordinary, often times they'll move in for a closer look. This time of year, all the resident deer that make up a given population, or herd, are very tuned-in to what's happening within the group. They've spent the whole summer together. All of the does know of each and every fawn and who their mom's are, and the same is usually true for the bucks. Sometimes the majority of a population can even be seen feeding together this time of year, bucks included.

Within many of these resident populations are big, dominant, record-class bucks. Though the percentages of pulling these trophy deer in to an early season fawn distress call are slim, it has happened. It's game calling. You never know exactly how an animal will respond, which is what makes this approach so exciting.

Because the cries commonly heard this time of year are from fawns – or does – under attack, throwing in a mix of predator calls can help. Try and simulate a coyote growling, snarling and yipping at a crying, struggling fawn, and this can definitely help to convince adult deer that they need to rush in for help. To create this range of sounds, I prefer using only one call, an open-reed, bite-down call. These calls allow you to easily regulate air flow and tone, whereby being able to very accurately mimic predators and prey.

On more than one occasion I've seen deer ward off coyotes and bobcats as they've tried nabbing their fawns. When it comes to protecting their own, deer can be very aggressive, which is why calling can be effective this time of year. If desperate to pull deer out of the brush, distress calls may be your answer this time of year.

Chapter Four
The Mid-Season
(October)

For the blacktail hunter, October is the month. During no other time of the year is so much happening, both for the deer and the hunter. The opening of multiple seasons, weather changes along with shortening daylight hours and major shifts in buck behavior make this a prime time to be in the field.

October also marks a time, because so much is happening, that is perfect to be out studying deer. The best part, the studying can be done while you're hunting. There is so much to be learned about the deer themselves this time of year, and being able to accomplish this while simultaneously hunting is an opportunity every serious blacktail hunter needs to capitalize on.

In this chapter we'll take a close look at what's happening with the deer this time of year, especially the trophy bucks. For instance, within the world of blacktail hunting, I think the least understood event is the rut, and in this chapter I'll share why I find rattling to be successful in October. Due to increased hunting pressure, October is also one of the most challenging times to kill a trophy buck. For this, I'll outline hunting methods that have worked for my family over the years.

Bottom line, October is a busy blacktail month. It's a challenging time to hunt, but a great time to learn.

Behavior

The month of October marks some of the greatest changes impacting trophy blacktail behavior. Early in the month deer go from a fairly relaxed lifestyle to being pressured by a sudden influx of hunters.

General rifle seasons usually open in October, roads that have been gated for 11 months are now unlocked, and a barrage of brush-beating, road-hunting fans take to the woods.

Smart bucks know exactly what's happening, and it only takes a matter of minutes for them to adjust to the unnatural events suddenly going on around them. In this short period of the opening day, bucks can go from living comfortably along the edges of their core area, to retreating into heavy brush, moving almost entirely under the cover of darkness. Often times, efforts to root out bucks from the brush only drive them deeper into hiding.

Once they feel the human pressure, the movements of trophy bucks become much more restricted. At this stage, each action of a buck is well thought out before being acted upon. This is the time of year that, rarely will a big buck appear anywhere by accident. He's typically very tuned-in to what's happening, and adapts accordingly.

Due to the ease of access through a vast series of interconnected logging roads, I feel the highest percentage hunts this time of year are for Cascade and foothill bucks. Mind you, getting a trophy buck is not easy, but so many people have access to so much land at this time, there are bound to be some deer that get caught by surprise. The interesting thing about these bucks, I'm convinced that you do not have to go to the deepest, darkest, most inaccessible chunk of terrain to find a trophy.

Let me give you a case in point. Two consecutive years in a row a buddy killed two record class bucks during the rifle season. Both came from the exact same piece of cover, quite low in the hills. The brush was only about 30 yards wide by 100 yards long. The deer were holding in a bush-choked grove of young fir trees standing about 20 feet tall, surround by freshly logged units on all sides and a main road that paralleled one entire side. It was so dense, it could only be penetrated on hands and knees.

He found this place by accident when he pulled off to the side of the road to let another rig pass. It was then he noticed a huge, fresh buck track. His buddy went into the brush while he walked around the backside of it. No sooner had he gotten situated on the edge when a big buck scampered out in front of him. He killed it with a perfectly placed shot. The next year they went in and did the same thing. It was an obvious big buck habitat, for when the first was taken out, another moved in. The most interesting part, I bet 100 rigs a day passed by each of those deer en route to "better" hunting grounds higher up in the hills.

I think because of the lifestyle blacktails lead, foothill bucks have a tendency to move around a bit more when compared with bucks in other regions. I believe the availability of prime food is so widespread and the overall cover so thick in this area, big bucks can wander a considerable amount of ground and feel safe. As the rut approaches, the large concentrations of does within this specific habitat also cause bucks to cover more ground, taking inventory on what's out there. Overall deer densities can be high in this area, too, which helps. As the month progresses, deer can even grow more active, depending on what's happening with the weather and surrounding hunting pressure.

October is a time when photoperiods shorten and weather changes. This means some of the bucks in the higher elevations start thinking about the migration to lower grounds. But even when the deer do start to move, it's usually in the dark.

One of the most interesting studies I've read was conducted by the Oregon Department of Fish and Wildlife in 1996. What it revealed was how highly nocturnal mature blacktail bucks truly are.

During this pre-rut study, multiple trail cameras were positioned along six known fall migration trails. The trails were leading from the higher elevations in the Cascade Range to lower elevation wintering grounds. A key to this study – which was cutting-edge technology back then – was the use of the infrared beams that triggered the camera's to snap a photo when and animal walked by, whereby recording the time and date of when an animal passed.

What they found was incredible, and confirmed what so many blacktail hunters have speculated for so many years. Of the 606 deer that were photographed, 87% of the bucks were caught moving at night. What's even more impressive is that of the bucks caught on film, 42% were 4x4s or bigger. These numbers prove that, even during migrations, most of the big buck movement is at night. They also confirm that there are some monster blacktails roaming the woods.

An interesting side note to this study is that 56% of the does and fawns traveled at night. That means nearly 1/2 of all doe and fawn

119

movement took place in daylight. This is important information to know because once does start moving, and the hormone production of bucks increases, the bucks will become more active during the day as their interest in does rise. This helps explain why sometimes bucks can be seen acting rutty, chasing does, in broad daylight in the middle of October.

Up high in the Cascade Range, where I've done a good deal of my October hunting, I've found that the bucks seem to be more solitary compared to blacktails in other habitats. I've seen some great bucks during this time frame, and all were either alone or with one or two other bucks. I don't think migratory bucks worry about keeping track of pockets of does like resident bucks do, because once several populations of does congregate in a major funnel, it's simply a matter of which does are in heat.

With that in mind, I do think any buck, no matter where he lives, will detect any doe that comes into estrus early. I've heard of blacktail fawns being born in the last week of April. Count back 200 days and that means the does would have had to been bred in early to mid-October. If there's one thing that can pull a buck out of his hiding place in broad daylight, in the busiest month of hunting, it's a doe. That's why I never totally rule out searching the back-trails of does come mid-October. Bucks might just be following them.

Sudden changes in weather can also get bucks up and moving. A good time to get after big bucks is right before or directly after the first heavy storms of fall. In some years, the first hard rains don't fall until October. One of my favorite times to be in the field in search of big bucks is right after a storm, when secondary food sources are made available. Mosses, lichens, woody twigs and nuts get blown from the trees, and bucks love eating these treats. I've seen, and taken, some very nice bucks in the middle of the day as I caught them out feeding the day after a big storm. At this time, the forest floor is moist and quiet, which makes stalking even more appealing.

It's a good idea to also monitor incoming low fronts and be sure to be in the woods during the "calm before the storm." Bucks are often active at this time, moving about in an effort to gather food before a storm hits. It's an instinctual behavior, as the deer aren't going to starve to death or die of exposure in their fairly mild climates. They just sense a storm is coming and their bodies tell them to prepare for it by feeding.

Moon phases are another weather-related factor to keep in mind, but honestly, something I've not paid a whole lot of attention to over the years other than a few, basic observations. The reason is, blacktail season is so short, and consequently I'm going to hunt regardless of what stage the moon is in. But one thing I have observed is that on a new moon, when the sky is darkest in the night, the deer are more crepuscular, that is, moving around during the early and later hours of daylight. Their level of activity can run quite high up until mid-morning, and then pick up again later in the afternoon. This means putting in more hunting hours during new moons can pay off.

Tracking lunar phases can impact blacktail hunting success.

During periods of full moons, when the night sky is brightest, I think there is more deer activity during the middle of the day than normal. I believe this is because the moon is so bright they feed in the middle of the night, then bed down early. Then, because they didn't feed as late into the morning as usual, they get up to snack around midday. They wont necessarily travel far to find food, but bucks will be up,

121

eating. During full moon phases, I'll stay out in the field all day long, hunting hard between the hours of 10:00 a.m. and 3:00 p.m., a timeframe when many people take breaks.

A big mistake I once made was heading into the hills too early one October day. I knew there were some big bucks around, and wanted to be in position to glass for them come first shooting light. There was a full moon, and rather than wait like I should have, I quartered down the hill to reach the spot I wanted to be. The moonlight was so bright there was no need for a flashlight to help see where I was going. Just before I got to my glassing point, I met a buck coming up the same trail I was going down. There was enough light to see the outline of his rack, easily a 150-inch frame. He ran off.

Rather than wait, I pushed on, and spooked another buck nearly the same size. My mistake, again. Had I been patient and waited until mid-day to go into that area, I would have likely found one of those bucks up and snacking. Going in early like I did was not smart, for I knew it would be too dark to get a shot. All I ended up doing was educating those bucks and blowing my chances of getting one. During the night, they'd obviously fed along the brushy meadows below and were making their way to their bedding areas under a full moon when I met them. I should have waited.

I have found that a full moon sometimes encourages deer to feed more into the openings at night, which means hunting the fringes at first light can be good, if you can get into the area without spooking them. I'm also convinced a full moon can put them more on edge, keeping them feeding closer to the safety of brush due to increased visibility. I believe where they feed during a full moon, and how far they're willing to risk traveling into openings is greatly impacted by hunting pressure and the number of predators in their area. One thing I do believe, is hunting them from above during a full moon is optimal as this angle of approach provides the best opportunity to slip in on a buck.

Be careful not to get directly above them, though, where sinking air currents will carry scent down to them in the early hours. Rather, come in from a quartering angle. This will allow you to see what's in front of you while keeping the wind away from the deer. Just don't make the mistake I did and get into the buck's territory too soon, it could cost you.

Once a buck beds down, if I can't see him, I'll try to avoid going after him in the mid-season. These bucks are already educated, and they know we're after them. They have multiple escape trails they can use, making the chance of getting a shot very slim. They're also pressed hard by natural predators as they prepare for winter. I rarely try hunting a buck in his bed, unless the situation is just right. When it is right, I don't push it. My goal is to sit back and watch for the buck, hoping to catch him as he gets up to snack or re-bed.

The biggest buck my Grandpa Haugen shot, a 216 pound 4x4 that sported an impressive 27 1/2-inch spread and scored over 150-inches, was taken from its bed. Grandpa made his way through a patch of ferns, and just as he got to the edge where the ferns met the timber, he noticed the tines of a rack sticking up above the pointed fern fronds. Slowly, he crept toward the buck. It didn't move. Grandpa got to within 20 yards of that buck – who obviously thought he was more concealed than what he was – and dropped him with one shot. This was the exception to the rule. Though bucks will hold and let you walk by, more times than not they'll bolt into deeper cover, never to be seen again that season.

Once pressured, I do think many big bucks will move a little higher on the ridge when bedding for the day. Often they'll let other deer bed below them, where they can detect potential predators. The dominant buck will usually bed looking downhill; keeping his back to the wind so he can smell any approaching danger.

Big bucks also bed in some of the thicker cover such as poison oak thickets, alders, ferns and a mix of brush surrounding fir and oak trees. Given their position and cover, this is why it's tough approaching a bedded buck. Then again, if all is right and the deer is approachable, go for it. Only you can be the judge of what to do at this time.

I have learned from the bedded bucks I've closed in on – either to photograph or try and shoot them – that my chances of getting close are much better when coming in from above and slightly off to the side. Again, this keeps the wind going across both of us, and deer just don't seem as flighty when approached from above as they do from below.

Regarding valley floor deer, you rarely get the luxury of approaching these bucks from above. They live on flat ground year-round, and in my opinion, the trophy aged bucks in these areas are the toughest to stalk during the month of October. I personally feel the bucks get ruttier later than other bucks, for the simple reason they know where most of the does and other bucks are, and who they are. This means they don't have to risk traveling around, covering much ground in search of does.

Another factor that makes tagging a trophy valley floor blacktail so difficult is they don't have to travel far for food. Big bucks go unseen for the simple reason that they can survive in a very small core area when need be. If they do travel to the edge of clearings to feed, it's often done well after dark. Remember, many of these deer are accustomed to being around humans 365 days a year, and when the season opens and they start getting pressured, they know exactly where to hide.

Coastal blacktails are as equally tough to track. As with the valley bucks, coastal deer have all they need in a small area, it's just that their home turf is much more rugged than that of their flatland comrades. Throw in thick brush, intense rain and driving winds, and it's easy to see why many hunters feel these are the toughest of all blacktails to get. They have a good argument.

No matter where you hunt blacktails this time of year, the older the buck the more restricted his movements will be. The bigger bucks are also more likely to be in thicker cover and they'll never be far from familiar escape routes. The key word here, routes.

Many times big bucks will utilize more than one trail. Telemetry studies have shown that blacktails only use the same trail on two or more consecutive days, 25% of the time. What's even more eye-opening to some hunters is that big, mature bucks rarely utilize primary trails. Instead, they travel along more covered routes, winding their way through brushy cover.

As for Sitka blacktails, most are still in their early season ranges, meaning you'd best be prepared to climb high in order to reach trophy bucks. A few might drop down if a bad snowstorm sweeps through, but as soon as it starts melting, the bucks are working their way to higher ground. For the most part, the timber-dwelling coastal Sitka blacktails are still hanging out in their primary comfort zones, since they are largely nonmigratory.

Glandular System & Communication

Be it through sight, sound, smell, even taste, deer communicate with one another in several ways. These are year-round forms of communication that deer rely on. A common misconception among hunters is that deer only communicate through scent use during the rut. While it's true that scent-based communication activity increases during the rut, it's also true that scent-based communication rises during the pre-rut period. This means October can be a time of heightened scent use activity among deer, something hunters can capitalize on.

The pre-rut period is an important time for bucks, and hunters. Personally, I feel the pre-rut is the best time of all to hunt, whereby offering the best chance of tagging a trophy buck.

Pre-rut, or the timeframe prior to the rut reaching its peak, is when bucks cover a great deal of ground in search of does in heat. I've found this to be particularly true among foothill, valley floor, coastal and open country blacktail populations. These are largely resident, nonmigratory deer that know their domains well, and most of the does within them. In an effort to ensure they gain first breeding rights, bucks will start cruising the country in search of receptive does. This activity starts well ahead of the majority of does actually coming in to estrus, which means it's also the best time for hunters to be in the field, trying to intercept these bucks as they move around.

So, where do deer scents come in to play in all of this? As bucks start actively seeking receptive does, they're also communicating with them through scent. They're also communicating with other bucks in the area. For hunters, observing how bucks behave when broadcasting odors through their various scent glands can unveil priceless information as to what state the deer is in, thus, what can be done to try and successfully hunt one.

We may not have the luxury of observing deer as they disperse scent, but that doesn't mean it's not happening. There are important clues to be aware of this time of year, clues that will show hunters where bucks are laying scent markers.

The scents deer use to communicate with one another are called pheromones. The actual word, pheromone, is based on the Greek *pherein*, which means to transport, and *hormone*, which means to stimulate. Pheromones are chemicals which trigger innate behavioral responses within members of the same species. There are various forms of pheromones, including alarm pheromones, sex pheromones, trail pheromones and many others that impact both animal behavior and physiology.

What hunters are most interested in is how deer use pheromones to communicate dominance, sex, sexual readiness and danger. This is usually done through leaving scent on the ground or surrounding vegetation by a process called self-impregnation, where they leave scent on their own bodies. There are multiple glands which deer rely on to produce scents, and some of these scents are so specific in what they're saying that other deer can decipher the specific deer which made them, no matter how many are in the area.

Every time a deer takes a step, it lays down a scent from its *interdigital glands*. Deer belong to the Order, artiodactyls; this means they have even-toed hooves, among other specific physical characteristics. The interdigital gland is located between the toes (or split hooves) of each foot, and carries an odor that can be strong enough for humans to detect.

I once came upon a fresh track in soft, moist soil. I knelt down, grabbed a handful of dirt and sniffed it. My buddy looked at me like I was nuts – nothing new. But when I told him it was fresh track, he really thought I was crazy. When I held out my hand and had him take a whiff, the look on his face was priceless. "You really can smell it!" he squeaked. We followed the track and caught up with the buck 15 minutes later, but he was too small to shoot.

My buddy, who had hunted deer around the country for years, never knew humans could actually detect the smell from interdigital glands. In the right conditions, you can, and it can help guide you when trying to decipher fresh tracks from old ones.

During the month of October, I think the interdigital gland is the most important of all, despite the fact deer use it to communicate with one another throughout the year. It's important now because as does go about their daily routines, and use numerous trails to get to where they're going, bucks will intently search these trails for fresh scent, then follow the does to see if they are coming in to heat. Ask any blacktail hunter, bow or rifle, what's the best way to get an educated, wise, trophy blacktail buck this time of year and almost every one of them will

126

tell you from a tree stand or at least a ground stand where you sit and wait. This is true because you're less intrusive for one thing, but also because you're elevated to watch key trails, the same trails you've concluded deer are using.

I've heard of many hunters over the years who, upon preparing to enter a stand, take the tarsal or metartsal glands from a deer they'd previously killed, tie them to their boots, then go walking through the woods. The idea is to allow the scent from the gland to mask human odors transferred to the soil from the boots.

This time of year, however, during the pre-rut period, I've had good success at getting deer to stick to the trail I walked in on or had to cross by using the interdigital glands of deer. Simply cut the glands out from between the toes – you may want to use rubber gloves, they're potent – and seal them well, then place in the freezer. When you're ready to go hunting, rub some of the oil from the gland on to the bottom of your boot, then tie the gland to a string and attach that to your boot, so it will continue leaving scent as you walk.

I've only done this a few times when hunting trails, and I believe it has worked. The deer have walked along the same trail I did, or where I had to cross it, sniffed the ground and kept going. The interdigital glands send the message of, "All is okay...if this deer passed through on this same trail, so can I." It also spurs bucks to follow the scent to find does as pre-rut progresses. This means using the interdigital glands of does to not only mask your scent, but to get bucks to follow it, makes perfect sense.

Have you ever watched a curious or spooked blacktail stomp its front foot on the ground? Every time they do that, they're dispersing more scent on the ground than when they simply walk. When bucks make scrapes – yes, blacktails have been known to make scrapes, more on this later – they also distribute large amounts of scent from their interdigital glands.

Interestingly, each deer has their own unique scent. This explains why it's the scent from the interdigital glands that does use to track their fawns, and why mature bucks alert others of their presence in an area. It's thought that perhaps some of the compounds in this scent may occur in higher concentrations among mature bucks.

Finally, since the molecules of these scents evaporate at different rates, depending on the terrain, weather conditions and amount of scent being secreted, deer can decipher which direction another deer is moving. The interdigital gland is an important one for blacktail hunters to know given the situations and conditions we hunt in. I feel it's even more important than in hunting mule deer and whitetails.

Just up the leg is the *metatarsal gland*. This gland – actually it's not a true gland due to the fact it lacks a duct – is located on the outside of a deer's hind legs, about half-way between the toe and the hock, or heel. Though the exact purpose of this gland is not well known, scientists hypothesize that it informs deer of each other's presence as well as warns of danger. Some believe that blacktails actually open the long hair surrounding this gland to alert others of danger.

I have noticed bucks flaring this gland when sparring or in tense situations of establishing dominance. Due to its location, I believe the gland is a form of communication that can deposit scent on long grass and on bushes as deer walk by, much like how the interdigital gland works.

Continuing up the hind leg is what I consider to be the second most important gland when it comes to hunting blacktails, and that's the *tarsal gland*. The tarsal gland is located on the inside of the hind leg, near the hock. These are true glands, capable of excreting oils, and are easy to locate due to the stiff, longer hair surrounding them.

Hunters consider this a gland of utmost importance during the rut, and I agree. The tarsal gland is used for rub-urination, or self-marking, whereby a deer brings its hind legs close together, slightly crouches, and then urinates. This allows the urine to flow down the inside of the leg, whereby carrying the scent of the tarsal gland to the ground. Bucks and does rub-urinate, though bucks really get aggressive with this gesture this time of year.

As with the interdigital glands, does can recognize their fawns by the smell of their tarsal glands, and vise versa. Does have also been known to rub-urinate, likely as a display of social status within a population. Bucks are known to use these glands to communicate their hierarchy and display their level of dominance. The lactones of the tarsal glands are so specific, they can reveal a deer's physical status, sex and age, which does take into account when looking for the right buck to breed with. These glands are thought to also be capable of giving off a warning scent.

In blacktail bucks, rub-urination begins during the pre-rut timeframe. It greatly intensifies as the rut approaches, resulting in a darkening of the hair surrounding the tarsal gland. The hair will also appear to be deep red in coloration, a sure sign a buck is telling the rest of the deer out there what he's all about. This is a key time for bucks to strut their stuff in an effort to establish a solid social ranking.

Without question, the tarsal gland is the most important when it comes to deer communicating with other deer. This doesn't necessarily make it the most important for hunters though, since we can't detect what's being "said" by each deer through their depositing of oils secreted from this gland. However, it is important for hunters to know what they're looking at when they see flared-tarsal glands or rub-urination in action.

Moving forward on the body, the *forehead glands* are next. These glands are located between the base of the antlers and the top of the eye sockets and are utilized most during the rut. Dominant bucks primarily use these glands by rubbing on trees and overhanging branches to display their age and social ranking.

The forehead glands excrete oil that makes the hair appear dark along the forehead region. The more intense the rut becomes, the darker a big buck's forehead can be. Bucks start making their presence known to does and other bucks through rubs on trees. They will start making rubs in October, during the pre-rut, and I've found many rubs during the second and third weeks of October.

Normally, larger rubs equal larger bucks, consequently if you start seeing small rubs early in your hunting area, just wait, bigger rubs should soon appear. If they don't, you may need to change hunting grounds if a record class buck is what you're after.

When rubs appear in areas with does, the chemicals released from the forehead glands can be so precise that it's thought to even synchronize the timing of the rut between bucks and does. It might also be used as a priming pheromone which can bring does into estrus. When you observe bucks rubbing their forehead glands on an object, it's for a reason, and it's also time to seriously start looking for big bucks.

Just in front of the eye is the *preorbital gland*. If you've ever caped out a deer for mounting, you've run across this gland. Many people think it's a tear duct. If you dig down into the recessed pocket in front

129

of they eyeball, you'll find this gland. It's almost woody-feeling in texture and carries a distinct odor.

The preorbital gland is actually controlled by muscles. Bucks can often be seen flaring this gland to signal aggression. Watch a buck closely through binoculars when it's displaying an act of dominance, and you'll see this gland flare up. I've seen it several times, and I've seen does open the gland when tending young fawns.

Bucks will deposit scent from their preorbital glands when making rubs. It's thought these glands may also express social status, and possibly help deer to identify one another.

Shifting to the deer's nose, the *nasal glands* are located in the nasal cavity of the deer. Not only does this gland keep a deer's nose moist so it can more easily detect smells, but it allows deer to leave scent behind. This is usually done when licking overhanging branches which is most commonly associated with bucks during the rut.

Salivary glands also leave the scent of deer behind, possibly through enzymes passed in the saliva. This scent is most commonly passed when deer lick or chew on branches, or rub trees. Of course, the number one goal of this gland is to produce saliva which contains digestive enzymes.

Keep in mind there are numerous glands within a deer's body, and they serve an array of purposes. If nothing else, it's good for hunters to see just how important these glands are for deer to communicate with one another. This, in turn, should reveal how acute a deer's sense of smell really is. Through learning how deer utilize these scents, hunters can combine the knowledge with observed deer behavior, and then do what's necessary to help take a trophy buck.

Hunting Tactics

The mid-season, though it's a brief timeframe, brings with it the most variety of ways blacktails can be hunted. This is largely due to the seasons themselves, which are set by each state's wildlife agency. But it's also due to deer behavior and even the tools being used for the hunt, be it gun, bow or muzzleloader. Knowing which tactical approach to take comes down to hunters being familiar with the land and how and why deer behave as they do at the particular time a hunt is taking place.

With those important aspects in mind, let's look at some of the most effective mid-season hunting tactics hunters can depend on to help take a trophy blacktail.

Party Drives

When it comes to hunting black-tailed deer, party drives are about as old-school as it gets, but this approach still works. This is the tactic I most recall taking place back when I could barely walk. Our party would pull into the hunting area well before daylight. Various activities, guided by flashlights and deep whispers saw hunt plans come together. Rigs would be shuttled and hunters strategically positioned for well-planned drives that were soon to follow.

Until I would be old enough to join in the hunts, I spent the early years – starting at age of two – in the truck with my mom, guarding the lunches. I still recall the level of anticipation with which I awaited the return of the hunters which involved listening for shots, yearning to hear their voices carry across the canyons, and hoping to see blood on their hands when they emerged from the brush. Party drives and all the camaraderie that came with it are what instilled the culture of blacktail hunting within me.

For our family, just about every season, more than one record book buck succumbed to these party drive hunts. There'd usually be an impressive number of tags to fill, and while not all the bucks were monsters, many were exceptional bucks, both in body and antler.

Though times have changed since I became indoctrinated to party drives back in the 1960s, the objective has not. The idea is to strategically place hunters on stands, and then have a group of hunters beat the brush in hopes of moving deer toward the awaiting hunters.

It's worth noting that members of party drives should wear hunter orange vests and/or caps, so they can clearly be seen by not only members in their own party, but by other hunters in the area. Ideally, it's best to conduct drives where no other hunters are found outside the hunting party.

Party drives are usually conducted in areas where you're looking for just one crack at a big buck, or hoping to flush any legal buck to put meat in the freezer. Once the old bucks know what's happening, rarely will they fall for the same trick twice in one season. And the more pressured they are, the more reclusive they become.

131

The great thing about party drives is that they can be employed just about anywhere blacktails are found. The first key is realizing that the objective is to kick these deer out of their bedding areas and safety zones, or intercepting them and moving them out as they make their way into bedding territory. The second key is trying to predict where the pressured deer will go. That's the hard part.

Knowing how a wise blacktail buck will react to pressure in the form of multiple hunters tromping through the brush is anyone's guess. It's interesting to note that back in the early days of party drives, just as many bucks were killed by the drivers as the hunters sitting in the stands. This is due to typical blacktail behavior.

When blacktail bucks are pressured, they flush, hold tight to the area or jump and try to circle back around from where they came. They don't want to leave their comfort zone until it's a last resort. Knowing the deer want to remain within their core area, hunters beating the brush can carry rifles with low power scopes, or no scopes at all, and be ready to shoot a deer when he jumps or circles around behind. Shots may come at close-range while deer hold tight in their beds, scoot between drivers or slip in from behind to re-bed. Before pulling the trigger, drivers toting guns need to make certain of their target and in which direction they're shooting relative to other party members.

When making party drives, things like wind direction and noise have little bearing on the hunt, other than the fact both can be used to spook deer from an area. The idea is to force the deer into a shootable position for awaiting hunters. Where the hunters can and will be placed is dictated by the lay of the land. From there, the group must figure out where the deer's bedding areas are, then how to get into the area so deer can be pushed toward awaiting hunters on stand.

How big of an area you drive depends on how many people you have beating the brush. We've had many successful party drives with only a couple people on stand and a few in the brush. We've also cleaned up on drives where six or more people surrounded the escape routes and had a dozen hunters tromping through the timber. Interestingly, we've also sent in one or two hunters 15-minutes behind the first wave of drivers, and had them kill big bucks that circled back around behind the initial wave of brush beaters.

One of the most important elements in putting together a good party drive is filling the gaps. The space between each person making a drive should be kept small enough so as to not allow any deer to slip between the cracks, unseen. In some open timber habitats, hunters may be spaced 100 yards apart. During some brushy drives, hunters may be no more than 20 yards apart.

I don't know how many times over the years, myself and many members of the team watched big bucks slither between drivers, with absolutely no chance of getting a shot off. As we tightened up the gaps during our drives, we ended up getting more shots at deer that held tight in their beds, and also kicked out more deer in front of us to awaiting hunters on stand.

Sometimes, the brush you'll push is so dense, carrying a gun is fruitless. Not only can it be dangerous carrying a firearm in such conditions, but getting off a shot in such thick bush is nearly impossible.

Combine that with the fact fellow drivers are burrowing into brush mere yards from you, and you can see that carrying a gun in tight-quarter drives is not always the best option.

When making party drives in deep canyons and along adjacent wooded hillsides with sporadic openings, be they natural meadows or logged units, think ahead. Often in these multi-habitat situations, multiple drives can be made in a single drainage over the course of a morning. Rather than making one big drive, dissect the country and see where you might be

Dense, small draws, like this, are ideal for one-man drives. Eleven deer were kicked out of this little willow thicket, including two nice bucks.

133

able to organize efforts into several smaller drives, whereby concentrating efforts on driving bucks from their core areas first, then from their likely escape routes. This may result in forcing deer out of each mini-drive, or pushing them into other safety zones where you can root them out again a drive or two later.

The important part in making any party drive a success lies in knowing where the deer are hiding and where their escape routes lead. We've had incredible success in stands of reprod no more than 20-feet tall, river bottoms so thick drivers carried shotguns stuffed with buckshot, deep canyons no other hunters cared to set foot in, and more. Play it smart, move through where the bucks are, let the wind and your noise carry to the deer, and just maybe you and your hunting partners can close the deal on a trophy buck.

One-Man Drives

At first glance, what appears to be the opposite of a party drive is the one-man drive. But in reality, the principle is the same: to force deer out of the brush. However, the approach of a one-man drive can be much more subtle, possibly even requiring a bit more forethought.

The success of a one-man drive comes down to knowing where a certain buck is, then wisely positioning someone on a stand, while a single person makes a drive through the brush in an attempt to push the buck out of cover. The biggest challenge of a one-man drive is making sure deer leave the area rather than hunker down in the brush or double back on you. The brush is usually so dense in a one-person drive, rarely does the driver ever get a shot at a deer. Their job is to push the buck out of there for the other hunter or hunters on stand.

The most important part of the one-man drive is selecting an area that can be effectively worked by one person. The same land you pounded with a party of six drivers is not likely the same ground you'll work with a single driver. Look for narrow corridors you can walk through, whereby being able to maintain visual contact with most of the possible escape routes a buck might utilize to worm back in behind you.

Typically, narrow patches of cover are ideal for the single-person drive. These patches may range in size from your living room to a football field. We've had success on solo drives in vine maple thickets, poison oak groves, reprod, thin strips of timber, willow thickets within river bottoms and creekbeds, narrow stands of timber bordering power line right-of-ways and logged units, ridgelines, the narrow end of funnels and more. But no matter where you choose to make a one-man drive, the most important element for success is usually the wind.

Unlike what we've been taught while employing spot and stalk tactics or selecting sites for a tree stand, on one-person drives you want to have the wind at your back. By having the wind blow from you toward the buck, you're able to use your scent as an aid in pushing deer from an area.

Some of the most successful one-person drives we've had came while slowly, quietly moving through the brush and letting the wind carry our scent to the deer. Often, when a deer smells you in these thickets but doesn't hear you crashing around and making excessive noise, they don't immediately bust out of there on an all-out sprint for the next nearest cover. Rather, they sometimes walk to the edge of their cover, survey their intended escape routes, and then make a move. This move may entail busting to the next best cover, holding tight, or slithering back behind the driver and burrowing in to where they just came from.

Then again, they are wise deer and there's never 100% certainty as to what they'll do. In some of the really thick reprod units these deer love to hold in, you can often see their feet and legs moving mere yards ahead of you. They know you're there, and you know they know you're there. There are no secrets in these tight-quarter drives. At this point it just becomes a matter of pushing the buck out of his protective realm, which isn't easy or always possible.

Once you know, or think you know, where a big buck is holding, assess the wind. From there, determine the direction the driver can come in for the most effective use of the wind to disperse his scent. Then place the hunter or hunters on stands where they'll be able to see the deer trying to make a getaway. Once the hunters on stand are in place, begin the drive. Be ready, it can happen quick.

Because some of the areas are so thick that you'll be driving, there's no surprising the deer. They know what you're trying to do and they are aware of where you are at all times. In this case, the most important part is getting the deer to flee in the direction of the hunters on stand.

For the person beating the brush, the most effective way to cover ground on a one-man drive is to zig-zag your way through the brush. Avoid hopping on the first deer trail you find and following it straight through to the end. Instead, walk back and forth, from one edge of cover to the next. This not only ensures that your scent will saturate the entire area, but that you'll cover every bit of ground.

Because the brush can be so dense on one-person drives, the driver is often forced to crawling on hands and knees. When this happens, look closely at the ground in front of you, trying to detect the movement of deer legs. You'll be amazed how close these deer will really let you get in thick cover.

One time a buddy and I were doing a one-man drive. It was my turn to sit. I was atop a little knoll and could see every inch of willow thicket my partner was walking through. He walked by the thickest part of willows and heard something. He looked through the brush and could see the back of a deer, lying down. It was too thick to walk through, so he picked up a stick and tossed it at the deer. Nothing happened. He picked up a rock and threw it. Still, nothing happened. He hurled a bigger stone at the deer and the brush erupted.

Three deer bolted from the little stand of willows, in an area no larger than a ping-pong table. The crazy part, I could see that patch of willows the entire time and never saw a deer until they ran. What's more, my buddy was less than 15-feet from those deer, and only could see part of one. It goes to show how tight blacktails will hold.

When they did finally bust out of there, they ran right through the creek bottom of dense willows my buddy had just walked through. They had pulled off the oldest blacktail trick in the book; let the hunter walk by, then squirt out the back door to safety. It worked, for there was a dandy shooter buck in the trio, but I never got a round off. They were simply gone too quickly, swallowed by thick cover.

When appropriate, tossing sticks and rocks can help in a one-man drive. The purpose here is to create noise that will push the buck from cover. This can be a good way of covering ground you can't get to on foot, or giving the illusion that there are two humans in the brush.

When in the thicket of a one-man drive habitat, pay close attention to sign. Look for tracks, rubs, droppings, multiple trails and which

136

direction they lead, beds, hair on limbs, antler sheds and anything else that will be an indicator that bucks are using the area. Once you get into some of these dense places of cover, it will boggle the mind as to just how much sign there really is, and how a buck even maneuvers in such tight quarters.

When you do find an area that holds a big buck, note where it is. If you kill a big buck from such a thicket, go back there again the following year. As I've said before, big bucks are rarely anywhere by mistake. These dense pockets offer big bucks what they need to stay alive, and if one buck finds it attractive, so will another.

Stands & Blinds

Many trophy blacktail hunters choose to hunt alone. As with some folks, most of my record book bucks came while hunting solo. For me there's no greater reward in the world of blacktail hunting than going one-on-one with a big buck, and coming out on top.

There are multiple ways a hunter can go solo in pursuit of big blacktails, and what a growing number of hunters are turning to are the use of tree stands and ground blinds. Since the topic of hunting from these devices was already discussed in the early season chapter, here we'll take a look at how using these tools relates to the mid-season.

October seasons primarily consist of rifle hunts. That means hunting pressure is high and big bucks are largely nocturnal in their movements to and from feeding areas. It also means hunters have to be smart in order to outwit trophy bucks. In recent years, rifle hunters have scored on some giant bucks from both tree stands and ground blinds.

The three most important elements to consider when hunting from stands or blinds are location, location and location. Simply put, location is everything when hunting from a stationary position. If you don't put yourself in a place to see big bucks, you'll never have the opportunity to shoot one.

Due to the amount of hunting pressure on public land this time of year, the most effective times to hunt from stands and blinds are the first and last couple hours of daylight. Actually, about the first and last 30 minutes of light are best, but I like getting in the stand early, to give things plenty of time to calm down. If hunting from an early morning setup, it should be placed in a setting that catches bucks as they move from their feeding to bedding areas. Remember, big bucks usually move out of feeding areas earlier than other deer, so you may need to situate yourself a good distance up the hill or into the brush, not simply near the entry point of a trail.

One morning I crawled into my stand two hours before first light. I was certain I hung the stand far enough up the draw to catch big bucks as they walked the trail across the little drainage from me. Two hours after the sun had popped up, all I saw were does and small bucks. On my way out of there, I glassed way up high, along the edge of some rimrock and found the three bucks I'd been targeting. All were bedded in the shade, overlooking the valley below. They'd all moved through well ahead of when I got in the stand. Had I made the effort to hang the stand another half-mile up the ridge, I bet I would have killed one of those bucks.

This time of year the bucks aren't as active as they are in the early season, at least not until the pre-rut kicks in. For this reason I like positioning myself up high, or fairly near the bedding areas. Where you position yourself depends on which of the blacktail habitats you're hunting in. Mind you, don't get too close to the bedding area for fear of educating the deer and altering their routine. But do get close enough to intercept the deer as they move toward their bedding territory early in the morning as well as catch them when they start moving down from their beds right before dark.

Because the big bucks are moving so early and late in the day, positioning yourself so you can see them is everything. The advantage here when compared to bowhunting season, is that rifle hunters have the luxury of long-range shooting. This means that setting up where you can shoot across a canyon or draw offers a better chance at seeing deer. Being able to see as much ground as possible is vital.

If hunting on private ground rather than public, that can be a different story. I've had a few excellent private land hunts – not nearly enough of them – and have learned these deer are less skittish than those on public ground. They simply aren't nearly as pressured, and as such, are comfortable to move about during the course of the day. On rainy or overcast, cool days in October, I'll sit in the blind or stand all day if I feel the need, and remain confident that I might see deer at any time.

138

As the month progresses, however, things change. Starting around October 23rd, I will stay in stands later in the morning and hop in them an hour or so earlier than normal for the evening hunt. This is because the pre-rut is about to kick-off, and bucks can start moving at any moment, on both public and private lands. The same is true for the migration in some areas, where bucks start vertically moving down the mountainside in search of better feed, and does.

Remember, one thing I believe is that the timing of the rut, and pre-rut, can change from year to year, area to area. It's important to be in the field as much as possible as the month of October progresses, so you can see exactly how deer are behaving. If you have multiple pockets of does picked out, late October is a good time to hang multiple stands or erect multiple blinds and rotate spending time in them. This will allow you to observe what's going on with specific deer populations, and hopefully catch big bucks as they start cruising for does.

For the rifle hunter, tree stands and ground blinds offer some very distinct advantages. Tree stands give you the benefit of viewing land, and game, from an elevated position. This means you'll be able to observe vast expanses of land and animals from one place that you'd otherwise not be able to see, without disturbing the surroundings. If you really want to study how animals behave in nature, this is the best way I know of.

Ground blinds afford a level of comfort, whereby allowing hunters to move around without being seen. If you're one who fidgets or can't sit still for a couple hours, ground blinds are for you. Blinds don't give you the green light to get careless, but they can hide movements which would otherwise be picked up in an instant, thus sending deer fleeing in the opposite direction. Good blinds are also nice because they are waterproof, adding even more comfort. Be sure to get blinds that are lined with black on the inside, to cover movement. You may also need to spray the outside seams and top with a waterproofing agent from time to time.

When it comes to watching game trails, there's nothing that matches the effectiveness blinds and tree stands have to offer. Not only do they allow you to watch and learn from nature, but they are comfortable, very efficient tools from which to hunt.

Spot & Stalk

If I had one way to hunt blacktails, it would be by spot and stalk. The buck on the front cover of this book is one reason why, and there's a great story behind him. What makes this buck so special is the fact that I didn't even pull the trigger, yet it was one of my most memorable hunts ever. I had an archery tag for later in the year, and my dad held a general season rifle tag.

Dad and I were together in southern Oregon. It was the first time either of us had hunted there, and what a pleasant surprise it was. The open country and abundant deer made it one of the most exciting blacktail hunts of our lives. It was a refreshing change of pace, being able to see more than 50 yards while blacktail hunting. We hunted both public and private land, and Dad ended up killing this buck on a chunk of private ground.

We'd seen the buck on day one of Dad's hunt, but couldn't get a shot. We started the day by going high, then glassing adjacent hillsides for buck movement. Plenty of bucks were spotted, but nothing big enough to take, not on day one. Then Dad located a little three-point. The buck was bedded on the upper end of a willow patch, and we searched hard for another buck that might have been with him. More than 10 minutes passed and Dad found another buck.

The look on Dad's face said it all. Dad's taken some great bucks over the years, and he said this was one of the better one's he'd ever seen. The buck stood and re-bedded so fast, I didn't even get to see him. This shows the value of having multiple eyes in the field so you can glass large tracts of land.

The willows were tall, so even if the buck did stand, there was no way of getting a shot from where we sat. We decided to relocate in hopes of getting a better angle on the buck. As we moved closer the wind changed, the buck busted us and he sprinted into a low-growing thicket of oak trees on a nearby hillside. I figured we'd never see him again. It happened so quickly there was no chance of a shot.

We continued walking our way down that willow-choked draw where the bucks were bedded, just to see if there were any other deer in there. We were actually filming a TV show, and had a couple other people along with us. While Dad and I walked through the willow thicket, one person stayed up high to keep an eye out for something we might miss.

The willows were 10 to 15-feet tall and ranged from five yards wide at the narrowest point to about 20 yards at the widest point. Once we made it into the bottom, we discovered the spring that provided year-round water for the wildlife and allowed the willows to flourish. We also found a labyrinth of deer trails like nothing I'd ever seen.

It was mid-October and dry. Not much rain had been falling. To the west of the willow patch was open hillside for 300 yards. To the east was the oak-studded hill the big buck had vanished into, about 50 yards from the edge of the willows. It was sparse, and if a deer ran out of there, we were going to see it.

Slowly Dad and I walked along and through that willow patch. It wasn't more than 150 yards long, and didn't take much time to cover. By the time we reached the end, we'd seen one doe. But when we hooked up with our buddy, he stated he had watched 11 other deer get up when we walked by, circle back above us and bed back down in the willows. They were in there the entire time and they let us walk right on by. He said some of the deer we were within five yards of us, but it was too thick for us to see them. Fortunately, no big bucks were around.

We returned each of the next two days, hoping to find the big buck, but saw nothing. Day four found us back there again, and this time we found what we were looking for. Less than 200 yards from where we'd first seen him, we spotted the big buck bedded in a poison oak thicket. Monitoring the wind and looking for other deer in the area that might blow our stalk when we closed in, we came up with a plan.

As we started making our way around the mountain, to come at the buck from the back side, a heavy fog moved in. This was a good thing, as it saved us over a half-hour of walking by allowing us to take a shortcut across an otherwise open hillside.

When we got into what we thought would be a good shooting position, we couldn't see the buck. The poison oak was too tall. We worked around for another angle, then another, and still saw no sign of the buck. More than an hour passed when finally, we spotted the tips of his rack. We'd been within 50 yards of him at one point, but he held tight. No doubt, he knew we were there, but he still held his ground.

Finally, the buck couldn't stand it any longer and took off. He ran straight away from us, downhill. Dad had no shot through the poison oak. Then the buck busted out in a small clearing at the bottom of the draw.

141

Dad already had his gun shouldered, hammer back. The moment the buck emerged Dad put the apex of the Trijicon scope where he wanted it, and the .300 Thompson/Center Pro Hunter chambered in Winchester magnum roared. The 180 grain Remington Swift Scirocco bullet found its mark and performed flawlessly, just as it always had on so many animals before and since.

The buck humped up, slowed, and fell over. It was one of the greatest moments of my hunting life. Dad made an absolute incredible off-hand shot on a running deer at 201 yards, then again, Dad always has been one of the best rifle shots I know. The best part, we caught it all on film for Outdoor America, a show I was hosting at the time on the Outdoor Channel. No, actually, the best part was that it was a father-son hunt on our favorite animal, and it was taken almost 31 years to the day from when I shot my very first blacktail, with Dad standing by my side. Dad's buck scored just shy of 150-inches, one of his best blacktails ever.

In this situation, persistence paid off. We saw the buck we wanted and stayed after him for four days. That's what spot and stalk trophy blacktail hunting is all about.

The author's father, Jerry Haugen, with his dandy open country buck that scored just under 150".

Though it's not always the best approach, spot and stalk hunting is what I was brought up with hunting out West; it's what I love. No doubt I've blown plenty of opportunities at bucks over the years because I'm always pushing forward and not observing enough, but I can't help it. I like to walk, cover ground and discover new things as I go. At the same time, I know I've killed big bucks I otherwise wouldn't have seen had I not been pushing myself.

Sure there are those days where I need to control myself and sit in a blind or tree stand to more effectively hunt an area. And there are days when I know deer won't budge from a spot, so drives must be organized. But I also know that covering ground allows me to learn more about the land, the habitat, the animals, and how they behave based on specific conditions they are currently encountering.

Though the spot and stalk approach is an aggressive one, it's not done carelessly. That means every move you make has to have a purpose behind it. I think that's one reason I like this technique so much, as it forces me to continually use my brain, which I definitely need help with.

Every decision you make when spot and stalk hunting must be based on conclusions you've drawn from what's been seen earlier in the day, or the season. Maybe it was the study of satellite images and topo maps which drove you to the area. Perhaps pre-season scouting missions led to the discovery of various does that now need to be monitored for buck movement. Maybe fresh tracks or a change in feeding area has led you to where you are. Perhaps trail cameras revealed something.

There are endless clues out there; the more keen you are on noticing them and then figuring out what your next step should be, the better your chances of scoring on a buck by way of spot and stalk. When hunting in this way, it's important to continually ask yourself, "What's next?" Then ask yourself, "Why?"

By figuring out which move to make next, and backing it up with sound reasoning, you're on the way to becoming a more skilled hunter on foot. With that in mind, there are specific things I do and look for this time of year which help me make smart decisions.

We know deer are pressured more now than at any other time of the hunting season. It's simple, rifle seasons are open and more people hunt with rifles than with other weapons. That's great, and whatever it takes to get people out in the woods, I'm all for it. Due to this pressure, big bucks alter their behavior from what it was a month ago.

Bucks will still be feeding, but most of their moving to and from feeding grounds as well as the actual feeding itself is done under the cover of darkness. This is what's commonly referred to as a buck "going nocturnal." But do they really go nocturnal? Do big bucks really sleep all day and become active only at night?

I think big bucks are more crepuscular than nocturnal, meaning they are active during the twilight ours of the day. They are also active at night, and sometimes during the day, which makes them metaturnal.

During daylight hours, deer lie down, nap, digest their cud, get up, browse a bit and nap some more. On hot days, they may even drink if living in an area where they can't derive ample moisture from their food sources. While the big bucks aren't moving about the forest like they do during twilight and nighttime hours, they are nonetheless, awake for select hours and somewhat active.

So, does this make them nocturnal? The term nocturnal has been used with blacktails for years, and more than anything I think it's used to describe when most of their migrations take place, along with most of their feeding once velvet has shed from their antlers. Rather than using the term nocturnal loosely, I like to think of day time buck movement this time of year as being more restrictive. In other words, bucks are awake and active during the day, though their movements have become more limited than what they were a month or two ago.

One October day I hiked into the Cascades looking for a big buck. It was general rifle season, fairly warm, dry and the forest floor was noisy. There was also a full moon. It took me some time to reach the 5,000-foot elevation point, but I finally made it. I was targeting migratory bucks, hoping to catch them prior to starting their march down the hills.

About 10:00 a.m. I spotted my first buck, a nice 3x4. A half-hour later I found two bucks feeding together. One of those was a shooter, well over 140-inches, but I couldn't get a shot off as they busted me. Around noon, I came across a fourth buck. He was bedded in a small strip of trees, in the shade. He was a heavy 3x4, and I'm still kicking myself for not shooting him. Instead, I watched him, hoping to get on a bigger buck later in the day.

I moved to the edge of the timber, within 100 yards of him. He could see me, and I knew it the moment I saw him lay his chin flat to the ground. I'd busted him in the open, and there was no hiding his rack that was pushing 18-inches tall and close to 20-inches wide. I sat, had a snack and glassed the area, hoping to pick up a bigger buck.

After not finding anything, I moved on, walking within 75 yards of that bedded buck. I continued past him, and he didn't move a muscle, not even a flicker of an ear. As I strode past, I kept looking back out the corner of my eye. Once I got about 75 yards past him, he lifted his head, stood, and ran into the timber I'd just come out of.

All four bucks I'd seen were over the 115-inch mark, and two over 130-inches. They were big bucks and they were up and moving in the middle of the day. I've seen this behavior on numerous occasions and it could be correlated to a series of factors.

First, I was way off the beaten path, and likely these deer hadn't seen any hunters this season. Second, it was a full moon, and I believe deer will often be more active in the middle of the day on full moons. Third, I was obviously close to their bedding area, which I believe is a big key.

Normally, I don't like delving too deeply into the bedding areas of big bucks. Doing so is risky as it can drive them out. I've done this many times, mostly on accident. If they are spooked from their main bedding locale, bucks will return, but when depends on how bad they were scared. On average, based on what I've seen, it takes a buck about three days to settle back down and feel comfortable in his bedroom. Then again, they may be so flighty that you never see them again.

On the day I went to the high country, I knew it was a one-shot deal. My time was tight, I wouldn't be back this season and I wanted a 140-inch buck or better. Knowing this, I planned my hike accordingly, taking me high into the ridgelines where bucks bed. What I found were three out of four bucks up and feeding during mid-morning. It goes to prove that though their daytime movements are limited, they aren't totally nocturnal. For the spot and stalk hunter, this is valuable information to know as it allows you to be in the field all day long and have the confidence of knowing bucks can be active. Just be careful not to push those bedding areas if it's a place you intend on coming back to hunt anytime soon.

When spot and stalk hunting this time of year, be aware that bucks normally are moving uphill in the morning, downhill in the evening. This means your time is best spent where bucks are traveling to, not from. The goal is to be ahead of where they are going, or glassing where they should be.

The spot and stalk hunter who aimlessly wanders into the woods hoping to chance upon a trophy buck may find success; then again, they may go twenty years without ever seeing a big deer. Pay close attention to all the clues that are out there and let them be your judge when it comes to making your next move. Patience and diligence are important, but not as important as playing it smart.

Tracking

When the conditions are right, it's possible to track blacktails, too. This skill is becoming a lost art in the blacktail woods, but there are some hunters who rely on it for finding big bucks. If this form of hunting can be pulled off, it's the ultimate blacktail accomplishment.

The idea is to cut a buck track, follow it, find the deer, make a stalk and shoot it. It sounds simple, but it's one of the most challenging feats in North American big game hunting. That's because cutting a blacktail track is not always possible in the terrain these deer live in, and when a track is found, how do you know it's an animal worth following? My answer to that, you don't, not always.

Of all the ungulates I've hunted around the world, I think one of the toughest tracks to decipher is that of a blacktail deer. Being able to tell a big buck from a small buck, even a buck from a doe can be tough to near impossible. I've observed literally thousands of blacktails over the years, and when I can, I try to study their tracks, tracks that I've just seen them make so I know what I'm dealing with.

What I've concluded is that it's not always possible, or easy, to decipher the sex of a deer based on its track. Sometimes it's obvious, other times it's not.

Take the buck on the cover of this book for example. We watched him and stalked in, jumped him from his bed and Dad killed him. After the shot we went and inspected his bed and the tracks he left in the surrounding grass. I would have lost a $1,000 bet right then and there had you told me that track was made by a buck, let alone 150-inch class

146

monster. Honestly, the tracks looked more like an average sized doe. Obviously, what I was looking at was the hind foot, which is smaller than the front, but it still boggled my mind as to how small it appeared.

Some blacktail tracks are tough to read. This one was laid down by a buck on the run, as witnessed by the author.

Generally speaking, a buck track is bigger than that left by a doe. Then again, the type of ground they're treading on plays an important part in helping to decipher what sex of deer actually left the track. In wet, soft ground, heavier bucks sink deeper into the soil. As a result, the pads spread out due to the pressure being applied.

When a deer runs on wet ground, a buck track appears even larger. But so will a doe. I've watched many does run across wet ground, then studied their tracks to find they splayed out just like that of a buck. To make it even more challenging, sometimes bucks leave dewclaw prints, sometimes they don't, sometimes does leave dewclaw prints, sometimes they don't. It's worth knowing that when dewclaw prints are made, those of the front foot are closer to the hoof than those on the back foot. This can help answer questions of sex in some circumstances, since the front end of big bucks are heavier than does.

On hard ground is where it becomes most difficult to differentiate between a buck and doe track. I've watched deer walk on the edges of gravel roads, along packed trails, in meadows and along numerous other types of hard-ground. What I've concluded thus far in my life is that it can be very challenging trying to tell the difference between a buck and a doe track on firm ground.

One of the biggest bucks I ever had the chance of shooting was one I tracked. I'd headed down a dead-end logging road, behind a gated, walk-in only area of public ground. Along the edge of the road was red dirt that was slowly turning to mud in the rains which had been falling all day.

I made it down to the end of the road, glassed the land below and saw nothing, so I walked back out. Just as I turned a corner, not 50 yards from where I'd been glassing, there was a fresh track, smack in the middle of my boot print. The rain was falling hard enough to drown my scent, but the track was plain as could be.

Looking closely at the track, I judged it to be an adult doe. It was pointed and the back parts of the pads were fairly thin. No question it was a doe.

Twenty yards up the road, I caught up with the deer, a handsome, dark-faced 4x4 that pushed 140-inches. I was bowhunting, and was so convinced the track was that of a doe, wasn't even thinking about shooting. When I tried coming to full-draw, the buck was inside 25 yards, and busted me. I shot anyway, and missed.

I felt so sick to my stomach I just about threw up. How could I have made such a mistake on a big buck like that? Thinking maybe the track I followed was that of a doe, and maybe the buck was following her, I went back to the beginning.

No question the track was small, and I was still convinced it was that of a doe. Then I pushed my finger into the pad print, expecting it to submerge in red mud. Instead, it hit hard rock just a fraction of an inch below the surface. The track stuck to the side of the road – in red mud – all the way up to where he jumped, dug in his dewclaws and pounced into the reprod. I continued along the trail, and the tracks he left in the softer mud were much larger, much deeper now that he was running on softer ground. There was no question it was a buck. It was the only track, and deer, around.

In the early 1960s a study of blacktail tracks in Oregon concluded that there is some overlapping of hoof size among bucks and does.

That helps alleviate some pain when misjudging a track like I did.

The study also showed the average front track of a buck to be just shy of 3 1/4 of an inch long, with a single pad measuring approximately 3/4 of an inch across. Add the other pad, then the spacing between the toes which can vary depending on the deer and the terrain the track is left in, and the overall width of a buck track will be near two inches wide, give or take a half-inch. Of course, this will vary, I've seen them smaller and much larger, but these are good, general guidelines to follow.

Bucks moving uphill are heading to bed, and likely left tracks in the early morning hours. These tracks will normally appear smaller than when the deer is heading downhill, which are left in the evening when going to feed. Because of gravity pulling down on the weight of the thick-chested buck, their tracks normally appear larger when moving downhill.

I've found rutting bucks that commonly walk with their head down and more aggressively than normal, will leave bigger splayed tracks at this time. This is due to the weight distribution with each step, and the fact they are moving forward with more kinetic energy. This is a good clue for October hunters to look for, whereby revealing when the bucks start acting rutty.

Under ideal conditions, it can be fairly simple to distinguish a mature buck track from a doe track. The hard part is finding consistently ideal conditions in the blacktail woods in order to do this.

If tracking, perhaps a question of equal importance to the sex is how fresh the track is. Many hunters, me included, have followed what appear to be fresh deer tracks, only to find they never end. Again, this comes back to the habitat blacktails live in. In some wet conditions, a week-old track can appear fresh.

On several occasions I've watched deer lay fresh tracks, and made it a point to check them each and every day for the next week or two. Sometimes the tracks get blown out by rain and look a year old after only a day. Other times, they look almost as fresh a week later as they did the day they were made.

Look for a glossy sheen with sharp edges to distinguish a fresh track in the dirt from an older one. As the track ages, its edges will break down and the shiny coating will fade. Also, look closely at any surrounding green grass or leaves they may have stepped on, to see if they've browned-up and started to wilt. If the vegetation is still fresh looking, chances are the track is very fresh.

Of course, snow offers the best conditions in which to track. If desiring to really test your hunting skills, head to the higher elevations when snows fall in October and track your deer. The amount of information you can learn at this time will no doubt make you a better blacktail hunter. One thing you'll notice is that because bucks have heavier chests and longer legs than does, they will routinely leave drag marks in the snow between each stride. This is done with the front legs. Their individual prints are much easier to distinguish in the snow, too, which makes tracking more enjoyable in such conditions.

Droppings are commonly found when tracking deer, and also hold important information. The droppings of bucks commonly clump together, whereas doe droppings are usually in the form of individual pellets. Deer will defecate up to a dozen times a day, even more. When tracking a deer and you happen upon some droppings, squeeze them to see how soft they are. If they are soft and easily break down, showing shiny hints of greens and browns, you're likely on a fresh deer. Keep in mind that the consistencies of droppings do change with diet and overall physical condition of the deer.

When tracking, look for the clues around you and study them closely. Be prepared to make mistakes, but more importantly, learn from them. I've been following blacktail tracks for many years, and still get on the wrong track. At that point, I take a bite of humble pie and move on.

Rattling & Calling

October means pre-rut, and it's never too early to start testing your rattling and calling skills. Depending on where you hunt, and what's happening within the population of deer you're hunting, rattling and calling can be productive in October. While does are not yet ready to breed, they are getting close, and that's all the bucks need to know.

Remember, hormonal changes within bucks are triggered by shortening daylight hours. This means a buck's brain automatically triggers testosterone production and release within the body at a certain time of year. With the production of the hormones come various factors which can release the hormones, causing bucks to become more aggressive.

Keep in mind that not all bucks will enter into an aggressive pre-rut at the same time, which means hunters who pay close attention to deer and how they are behaving will stand the best chance at filling a tag. In recent years, however, I have noticed what I think to be earlier pre-rut activity among bucks in the 500- to 1,000-foot elevation range, in particularly in the coastal bucks and the foothill bucks. I think the primary increase for rutting activity in these places, this early, comes down to DHLS. Not only has DHLS decreased the number of does in an area, but because bucks are more prone to this disease, their numbers have remained stable, overall, in some regions.

This means the competition among bucks is greater, which I believe causes pre-rut behaviors to kick-in earlier than they used to in these areas. I have no scientific data to support this, only my personal notes taken through years of observation. Two to three years after DHLS has swept through an area, and it's made its way into many of my hunting grounds, I've definitely noticed a decline in doe numbers. At the same time, food and water sources have remained stable, which has kept the bucks in the area. The result is higher buck-to-doe ratios, thus more competition for what does are in the area.

It also means that because there are more bucks, and fewer does, the bucks have to cover more ground in search of receptive does. I've noticed them starting to check out does earlier than they used to, up to three weeks earlier than when populations were healthy. In an effort to keep track of does and see which ones may slip into estrous early, bucks have to cover ground.

These bucks still live within their core area, but the periphery of this territory will definitely change as photoperiods shorten. For hunters, finding such movement can be a gold mine.

When you do find bucks in pre-rut behavior, that is, cruising around, sniffing for does, making rubs and scent markings, take note as to location. The first thing I note is the elevation. When pre-rut activity kicks in, I've found a strong correlation tied to the elevation at which it's happening. In other words, if it's occurring at 750 feet elevation in the Coast Range, that's the same elevation, in which I'll concentrate initial hunting efforts in the foothill region. Then again, I don't use this as a steadfast gauge, for it can change, too. If nothing else, it makes a good starting point from which to begin a hunt.

151

This is what makes hunting blacktails so challenging, in that you can't put them into a neat little capsule and assume that what's being observed at one point will happen the same time next year in the same place. For that matter, you may find bucks engaged in pre-rut behavior in one drainage, and then travel a few miles away while remaining at the same elevation, and not see any sign of bucks acting rutty. That's blacktail hunting, and is an example of why these are the toughest of all North American deer to consistently attain.

I've observed bucks in heavy pre-rut on several occasions, from October 15 through the end of the month. Once I see a buck acting rutty, I know he's going to be aggressive and covering ground. The pre-rut is one of the best times to locate big bucks, as this is when they are on the move. Once the peak of the rut hits, bucks may settle down with pockets of does hidden in thick brush, and may never be seen. This is why the pre-rut can be one of the best times to take a trophy blacktail.

Another place I've observed pre-rut behavior early in the year is in California's high country. Specifically, I've seen it, and heard a great deal more about it, as these bucks migrate to lower elevations. Rutting behavior can be observed in these deer in early October, and can increase as the month progresses. These high elevation bucks drop down in elevation earlier than Cascade blacktails do, I think due more to a lack of good feed than anything, thus explaining why I've never observed any major pre-rut behavior among the Cascade blacktail populations until a bit later.

The frustrating part about the pre-rut is it can turn off as quickly as it starts. Multiple bucks may be seen running crazy for a couple days, then nothing. This is normal, for what they're discovering is the does aren't in heat, thus aren't worth wasting energy on. Instead, the bucks will keep feeding, trying to amass as much body weight as they can for the upcoming rut and winter.

But just because the pre-rut may shut down doesn't mean the bucks won't act aggressive when given the chance. If you observe a buck acting rutty, or hear reports of bucks cruising for does in October, take that as an opportunity to be aggressive yourself. Rather than taking a passive spot-and-stalk approach, try rattling and calling in these areas of increased buck activity.

**Haugen has rattled and called in many
bucks during the mid-season.**

When I set up to rattle and call in areas during the pre-rut, my approach is different than later in the year. Early on, bucks are covering more ground than they will be in a few weeks, so my rattling sequences are not very long. Typically I'll rattle 10 to 15-minutes, maybe 20 if the situation calls for it. Then I'll move to a different area and repeat the sequence.

The idea is to cover ground, just like the bucks are doing. This means the chances of locating them are greater, since they simply may not be able to hear you if calling from one vantage point.

In early rut, I might set up and call in four or five places along one drainage. Now, if I were to go back into that same area during the tail end of the pre-rut, or in the early stages of the prime rut, I would only call in one or two places. But because the pre-rut finds bucks covering more ground, I want to do the same in hopes of finding them.

When rattling and calling from Mid-October through the end of the month, my sequence is different than it is a week or two later. Often I hear of people using a rattling sequence and religiously sticking to it. Personally, my sequences change throughout the course of a hunting season to fit the behavior of the deer. In other words, I observe

153

deer behavior and base my rattling and calling on what they're doing. Not only does this change from mid to late season, but it can also change from one day to the next.

Though bucks are capable of covering a great deal of land during the pre-rut, it doesn't mean they're at the height of their aggressive behavior. In fact, they still have a long way to go as testosterone continues to build up in their bodies. This means that though they are growing aggressive, they're not at the peak of their aggressive behavior. Understanding this is important.

When I call and rattle during the pre-rut, I don't do it with near the aggression I do later in the season. I don't bust branches, rake trees, tear up the ground or do much grunting, usually. Instead, I concentrate my efforts on non-aggressive rattling and doe bleats.

Before bucks engage in life or death battles, they enter a stage where they size-up one another. This is a time when they'll lock antlers and get into light sparring matches. The purpose of this is to start establishing a pecking order without risking injury. Many times simple posturing will yield a result, without there ever being a need to lock up racks.

During this time of year, once I see bucks cruising and acting aggressive toward does or other bucks, I'll get setup in the area, either upwind or in a cross-wind situation, and start with some light rattling. Because I don't want to risk spooking a deer out of the area by way of intimidation, I'll start off with soft sounds. Such sounds are best achieved with natural antlers, either sheds or antlers that have been cut off of a previously taken buck. I've also had good results with some rattle bags this time of year, but avoid pounding them too hard, so as not to create too much noise.

I'll rattle softly for 45 seconds to a minute, then sit and watch for a couple minutes. If nothing shows, I'll do the same, only a little louder this time. By the third sequence, if nothing shows, I'll throw in some doe bleats. If nothing shows, I'll continue rattling for about a minute, with a two to three minute break in between. About every third sequence I'll include some doe bleats, just to let bucks know there is a doe around.

I've called in several bucks this time of year without even rattling. This is where doe and fawn distress calls can work very well. This is a

154

time when fawns are starting to be weaned from their mom as she prepares for the upcoming rut. Behavior among fawns and their mom is bitter-sweet this time of year, for they verge on splitting up one minute and maintaining their bond the next. This often results in fawns bawling to locate moms, and vise versa. Using these distress calls will often attract the attention of other does, and bring them in. Often times, as these does come to inspect what's going on, they'll bring in bucks with them. Then again, I've used bleats to have only bucks respond. You never know what will happen in the blacktail woods, especially if you never try.

If, after about 15 or 20 minutes of calling in one spot, I get no response, then I'll move on. If I primarily rattled in the first few spots, I might switch it up and do more doe talking in the next setup, just for something different. This is especially true if there are good numbers of does in the area.

The key to rattling and calling success this time of year is based on deer behavior. Watch what the bucks are doing and where the does are hanging, and base your approach on that. As behaviors change among these deer, adapt accordingly.

Keep in mind that though rattling and calling this time of year is effective, it's not near the high-percentage proposition it will be in a few weeks. But you never know unless you try. There are some big bucks killed every year from October 15th through the end of the month, during the pre-rut. Whether they were called in or shot while acting rutty, both cases prove that there are key shifts in buck behavior this time of year. The important part for the trophy hunter is to recognize these changes and adapt their hunting approach to fit the situation.

Chapter Five
The Late Season
(November - December)

For many blacktail hunters, the late season usually encompasses the time frame from the peak of the rut to end of the season. But for me, late season starts the first of November, and this is solely based on deer behavior.

Beginning around Halloween, there's a definite shift in buck behavior amid the blacktail's overall range. Mind you, this shift — the rut — isn't always consistent, meaning it doesn't necessarily happen within every given habitat blacktails occupy at the same time. But overall there is a change in buck behavior, and hunters can use this to their advantage if they pay close attention.

The late season sees many forms of hunting. It's the tail-end of various general season rifle hunts, and the start for late season archers. For some youth, November marks the beginning of some of the best special-draw blacktail deer hunts imaginable. Then there are those front-stuffer fans, hunters who can't wait to head into the hills in an effort to fill their muzzleloader tags.

The opportunities are many during the late season, and success often boils down to recognizing how deer are behaving within your hunting area, and more importantly, how you choose to hunt them based on this behavior. That's what this chapter is about.

Behavior & Habits

By November first, most blacktail bucks are thinking of the rut. Simply put, the rut is a time of breeding, when does become fertile and accepting of bucks, and bucks become sexually active and physically aggressive. Whether they're in pre-rut mode or getting close to peak-rut status, there's no question, a buck's hormones are telling him it's time for the breeding season. Now, more than any other point in the year, buck behavior is based on what the does are doing and how other bucks in the area are acting.

Populations of bucks living in the high country are thinking of the migration as much as they are the rut. Then again, some migratory bucks have so much food available, their only concern is breeding does. For these bucks, long winter migrations may not happen. Instead, these bucks can drop a few thousand feet in elevation in only a few days, do the breeding they yearn for, then return to the high country a couple weeks later to live in solitude until next breeding season.

For bucks that have already migrated to lower elevations to escape snow and find better food, their quest now becomes to find does. For the more resident bucks, those hanging in the foothills, along the valley floors, amid coastal forests and in the open country, they have all their needs being met. Food, water, shelter, multiple trails and escape routes; it's all in place. The only thing that's changed for these bucks is an influx of more deer, both bucks and does.

Based on the dynamics of what's happening around them, bucks are now on full-alert. During the times when early migratory bucks make their way into the territory of resident bucks, I've observed rut-ting activity happening earlier than normal. I've talked with several seasoned hunters who believe the same.

A neighbor, who has scored on many big blacktails, doesn't even pick up his rifle until the last few days of the season. One season, not long ago, he'd done his homework and found several pods of healthy does. He was hunting about 1,000 feet in elevation, in the foothills of the Cascades.

After work he'd head out to hunt the last couple hours of daylight. He hoped to find bucks with the does, and kept checking each doe herd, sometimes twice each afternoon. The first three days he didn't see a buck. Then, with two days remaining in the season, he found a nice buck chasing a doe through a vine maple thicket.

The first thing that caught his eye was how the buck was behaving – head down, every step being guided by his nose. Then he saw the buck's rack. He was looking down on the buck, and wanted to get a

Tim Wright downed this handsome record book buck after he caught it acting rutty toward the end of Oregon's general rifle season.

good look before pulling the trigger. He moved ahead of the deer, and when the buck followed a doe out of a thicket, he finally got a good look at him. It didn't take but a few seconds and a shot rang through the canyon. It was November 3rd, and my buddy had just filled his general season rifle tag on a 137-inch 4x4.

During those last couple nights of the season, there were several good bucks taken at this same elevation along about a 50 mile stretch of the Cascade foothills, a testimony that the rut was happening in this specific range. Actually, it was more likely pre-rut that was spiking, as bucks suddenly appeared from nowhere. These big bucks often venture out on excursions, where they'll enter territory they've not been in all year. These excursions can find bucks moving across or down ridges a distance of a mile or two. Bucks will go on these excursions during pre-rut as well as peak rut. If you see a monster buck one time, then never see him again after a season or two of hard hunting, chances are, what you saw was a buck on an excursion.

When you see bucks moving like this, it's like the gates were opened and big bucks let into the breeding pens. The does were always there but the bucks just started showing up. I've seen impressive appearances like this among each of type of blacktail, but it seems especially high amid Cascade, foothill, open country and valley floor bucks where timber patches prevail over river bottoms.

As the pre-rut continues this time of year, look for bucks to cover more ground than during the rut. This is one reason it's wise to hold out as long as you can, for fresh bucks can pop up anywhere, anytime at this stage in the season. Bucks are covering ground in search of does, and does are entering into estrous. It's that simple.

Once they've found populations of does, bucks will periodically return to check their status. Once one doe comes into heat, a buck will usually stick close to her, knowing other does in the group will soon follow. When this transition happens, things can get very exciting. The important part is for hunters to recognize when the transition from pre-rut to peak rut kicks in.

One season I sat in my tree stand for three days, and saw one buck. My scouting had led me to hang a stand on a timbered knob, where multiple trails intersected. There was a drainage off to each side and plenty of does in both areas. Prior to my late archery season opening, I spent plenty of time scouting and watched bucks move back and forth across this ridge, checking on does in each canyon.

On day one I entered my stand at three in the morning, and sat until dark the next evening. I didn't see a single deer. Day two found me back at it, and I had one little three point pass by. Day three was a repeat of day one, not a deer. By the last hour of day three I'd had enough. I knew cougar populations were high in the area, and figured maybe a cat had driven the deer out of the area. I'd seen it happen several times before. I was also on public land, so maybe other hunters were in the area.

Frustrated, I climbed out of the stand and hiked down into the canyons to try and locate any does. Within the first 15 minutes I laid eyes on three giant bucks, not 200 yards from the stand I'd sat in the last three days. One was a giant buck, over 150-inches, the other two each over 125-inches.

"How could I have been so stupid?" I thought. The bucks had gone from pre-rut to peak rut right before my eyes and I failed to even recognize it. I just sat in my stand, hoping, instead of thinking.

Some quick glassing confirmed the does were still in the area, as were bucks, plenty of them. The buck that had been cruising back and forth, horizontally across the ridge, was now hooked up with does in heat, and had no intention of leaving them. In retrospect, it was so obvious, and I kick myself for not recognizing it.

If there's one thing I've learned over my years of hunting black-tails, it's that when bucks enter into pre-rut and start covering ground,

their travels largely take them horizontally across the hills. Rather t[...]
drop and lose elevation, bucks make a deliberate effort to seek out does
hanging at the same elevation line. I've seen this with rutting bull elk in
the high country as well, where they stick to the same elevation to find
receptive cows.

With blacktail bucks, they are searching for does who have come
into heat, and they do so by either working horizontal benches or crossing
ridges and checking out brushy draws where does are known to hang.
However, another very important behavior I've observed is that once
the rut kicks in, that is does in a specific group come into heat, bucks
will stick with them, hanging in that specific drainage. At this time,
bucks abandon their horizontal movements connecting food and shelter and stay with specific groups of does. They will move up and down
that draw and into smaller draws that may hold does, but it's not often
they'll leave the area until most, if not all, of the does have been bred.

Recognizing these shifts in behavior is important for the late season hunter. As I recovered from my mental lapse of sitting in a nonac-
tive stand for three days, I watched as bucks chased does. Seeing an
opportunity, I moved in for a shot. The deer were on the edge of a
clearing, running does in and out of a stand of 20-year old reprod. My
tactic was simple. When the bucks chased the does into the thick stuff,
I'd move forward. It worked, and in less than 20 minutes of stalking, I
arrowed a Pope & Young buck in the waning seconds of daylight. He
wasn't the 150-inch buck I'd seen, but a buck I surely was not going to
pass up.

I didn't regret shooting that buck, but lying in bed that night I
couldn't help but question my decision to shoot. There's no question
the bucks had hit peak rut the day I entered into my stand, as was
evidenced by the sudden lack of movement. This meant that the likelihood of that big buck moving out of the area was slim, since he was
obviously the king of the hill. I bet I could have let them be, slipped
back in there the next day and had a crack at that big buck. Then again,
I'll never know.

Once the does in a given group are bred, a buck usually goes back
to cruising the land in search of more does. This is what I call the
post-rut period. Though bucks are still rutting, they're not locked down
like during the peak rut. They simply are on the move, similar to the
pre-rut, though not as intensely.

161

By the time of post-rut, which can be anywhere from mid-November to late December, bucks are usually tired. They've starved themselves, they've been beaten up and they've lost a considerable amount of body fat. Still, they're driven by the innate desire to pass along their genes to as many does as possible; it's just that they may not be as aggressive as they were a couple weeks prior.

In populations of Cascade, foothill, coastal and open country deer, I've noticed a pattern where, once the peak rut is over, bucks start moving horizontally once again. This means they try to cover a great deal of ground in search of does that were missed being bred in their first cycle.

Another thing I've noticed, while these bucks are willing to cover a great deal of real estate, they don't do it as quickly as they did during the pre-rut. While I've seen a buck chasing a doe early in the morning during the post-rut, and observed that same buck late in the day inspecting other does well over a mile away, his actions in both cases were less aggressive. He was there, but had no challengers, and wasn't going to be pushy about it. He simply waited, patiently, with both groups of does. He even fed a bit here and there.

I watched this buck closely in the morning, and again in the evening, with another group of does. He was one I wanted, as his rack would have easily added up to 140-inches of antler. But there were always too many alert does looking around. Twice I thought I had a chance, and both times were when the buck was bedded down. Once a change in the wind gave me away, and the other time, a leery doe, but the point is he bedded down, in mid day, twice.

Because bucks are tired late in the season, they try and get their bodies rest when they can. Sometimes they'll stick with a group of does, hanging on the outskirts until a doe comes into heat. Sometimes they'll run checks on multiple herds of does, hoping to find a receptive doe. In between and even during these times, bucks will routinely bed down at this stage in the rut, giving hunters an opportunity to move in for a shot.

At the extreme end of the post-rut is total shutdown, where bucks simply give up on chasing does and go back to feeding. Once this happens, bucks melt back into their core areas, actually into the nucleus of their core area. At this point, all they need is food and shelter. By late winter, blacktails usually get all the water they need from their food sources, unless, of course they are living in a very dry climate such as in parts of California. This means their movements are very restrictive, and deliberate.

The production of hormones has slowed, at this time, and big bucks have regained their common sense. The end of post-rut is one of the most challenging times to kill a trophy blacktail simply because their movements have become so limited.

When hunting the very late season, at the end of the post-rut, you'll need to delve deeper into the core area of big bucks. This is risky, for they're back on full-alert and know they are vulnerable to predators after having just come off the rut. They expect danger and look for it. For the archer, this is a very tough time to fill a tag, and your best bet often lies in setting up a stand or ground blind near a buck's central home and hope to catch him during a period of activity. Just be careful not to bump a mature buck from deep within his core area this late in the year, for they may not return until well after the season, when it's time to start dropping their antlers.

If you have the flexibility of hunting a variety of terrains during the late season, post-rut is a good time to head into the upper foothill regions in hopes of intercepting bucks as they move back into their core territories. These aren't necessarily migratory bucks, rather bucks that have dropped in elevation to capitalize on the rut. Often times, these bucks can be caught slowly making their way back up the hill where their intent is to carry out a secretive lifestyle until next summer, when their racks are covered in velvet and they are once again forced into the open.

With the pre-rut, peak of the rut, and post-rut all happening during the late season, there's a great deal of behavioral information hunters will want to be cognizant of. Observing how deer behave, and understanding why, can answer many questions as to how you should go about hunting them.

Knowing what to do, when, is important when hunting trophy blacktails. The great thing about hunting the late season is it often affords you multiple tries, which means its okay to make mistakes.

There hasn't been a season that's gone by where I haven't made a mistake, or several mistakes. Okay, there were two seasons where this didn't happen, but those were the exception. One was when I killed my very first blacktail minutes into opening day, the other when I arrowed a big buck after sitting in a blind for only two hours. But those hunts are the exception rather than the rule, and having hunted these deer for so many years, I can appreciate the easy ones when they come.

With certain buck behaviors in mind, and knowing they are largely based on does this time of year, let's take a look at how to most effectively hunt them. What I like most about the late season is that hunters can be aggressive, make mistakes, learn, and still have a chance of tagging a trophy buck. There's no better time to be afield, try new things and study the behavior of trophy blacktails. Of course, the more we learn, the better hunters we become.

Rattling & Calling

Since I covered my pre-rut rattling and calling approach in the previous chapter, let's get right into peak rut rattling and calling techniques. Because things have stepped up a notch in terms of aggressive buck behavior, now is the time for hunters to do the same.

Whether you're rattling and calling from a tree stand or off the ground, the peak of the rut is a great time to do so because bucks are so defensive of other bucks in their area. They are also curious to see what they can hear, which makes calling even more effective. I think it's the nature of the dense brush blacktails live in, but for whatever reason, they are eager to see what's making sounds in their territories. I've found this to be true with blacktail wherever I've hunted them, from Alaska to California.

When I go in to an area I want to rattle, I make sure of the wind direction. Nothing gives a blacktail hunter away more quickly than the wrong wind direction. Ideally, I like setting up where I can call into a steady crosswind or a headwind. Many bucks will walk directly toward the sound of a fight before starting to circle it to catch a scent, which makes hunting into a crosswind quite effective. If the winds are swirling, I'll get into canyon bottoms and rattle from a more protective environment or head higher on to a ridge line where winds are consistently moving in one direction.

In most situations, I like getting about a quarter of the way down a hillside before I start rattling. This will allow me to continue working my way all the way down to the bottom of the drainage as I go, which can result in being able to rattle from different positions. Normally, this scenario takes place when I know there are does in the drainage, and I'm trying to locate bucks that may be with them.

When hunting in smaller drainages, I may work horizontally, from ridge to ridge, rattling as I go. In the high country, when calling amongst migratory deer, I'll usually try and locate the deer themselves, or at the very least, fresh sign, so as to narrow down my search. If I'm calling on river bottoms and along valley floors, I'll concentrate my efforts where I have most recently seen groups of adult does.

Before I begin my peak rut rattling sequence, I gather a couple important items. I'll get an arm load of branches and a club. The branches are about the diameter of my thumb, and are crisp so they'll make a good cracking sound when I break them. The club is sturdy, about the size of a baseball bat. Once these two items are in hand and

I've chosen a rattling site, I'll settle in.

How long I rattle in an area depends on the situation. There's never a set time, or a set number of sequences. Think about it, deer don't battle for a set time, and then give up. How long they battle depends how well matched up they are, what's at stake and how good of shape one or the other is in. Bucks whose antlers get locked-up may make racket for days. If a

Later in the season, Haugen's rattling strategy becomes more aggressive.

165

dominate buck fights with an insubordinate buck, the battle may last less than 30 seconds.

I've rattled areas for over two hours, others less than a minute before filling a tag. In one area, good friend Bret Stuart and I hiked into position early, well before first light. A heavy mist made for quiet walking which was ideal for getting to where we needed to be. We were atop a wooded knob, surrounded by roughly 20 acres of 40 year old timber and lots of sword ferns. The knob was surrounded by various ages of logged units, all of which held plenty of food, thus good numbers of does.

It was late season and the rut was going. We sat in that spot for over two hours and rattled in four different bucks. The first buck to come in was the biggest, and he winded us. The fourth buck that came in was also a nice, mature buck, and one we should have had, but just as I anchored he busted me and took off. The lesson here, don't give up rattling to early if you feel any bucks are in the area. This is especially true if there is little bedding habitat to hold a large density of deer.

With stick and twigs in-hand, I select a place which offers plenty of shooting lanes no matter what weapon I'm hunting with, or if I'm calling for a fellow hunter. Blacktail country is brushy, and one thing I've learned through many errors is that wise bucks rarely take the path of least resistance. Not always will they come in on the trail you thought they should. More often than not they come in cautiously, surveying their surroundings as they approach. Then again, they can be very gullible this time of year.

If it's been raining, the ground is wet, or I'm in big country, I prefer synthetic rattle bags during peak rut. This is because I'm after volume more than actual sound replication, and synthetic bags produce more sound than real antlers. Mind you, I don't get lazy; I still want a rattle bag that produces a good, rich tone. There are a few good ones on the market, and others that should be melted down into children's play toys. Experiment with a rattle bag before getting one. My favorite is one manufactured by BowTech.

Again, sound is more important than authenticity this time of year. I know of guys who have rattled in trophy bucks with empty water bottles, pop cans and grunts made with their voice. One time on Kodiak Island, I saw a buck moving and didn't have time to dig into my pack

166

for the rattle bag. I quickly grabbed a handful of dead, hollow devil's club and started banging and busting them apart. The deer stopped and moved right toward me. He came within range, but one of his antlers was busted off, so I let him go.

When I start rattling, I do so fairly subtly. Though it's peak rut and the deer are amped, I've scared way too many deer that were close to me by starting out too aggressively. I'll rattle lightly for about a minute, simulating deer that are touching antlers in an effort size-up one another. In my experience, this has kept more deer around, rather than spooking them out of the area.

I'll then take a break for about two to three minutes, and then rattle again, this time a little more aggressively. Again, I'll wait a few minutes, arrow nocked or gun shouldered and set on shooting sticks. These bucks can appear as an image before you so fast, you have no idea how they got so close without your seeing them. This is where blacktails earn the nickname, ghost of the forest.

If nothing shows up after the second sequence, my third series is all out aggression. I'll hit the bag hard, making certain to produce non-rhythmical sounds that sound like fighting bucks, not a person going through the motions of hoping to fool a buck. When bucks fight, it sometimes results in death. These fights are very aggressive and bucks are often injured to the point where they're put out of commission for the rest of the breeding season. Keep that in mind when rattling at this stage in the season.

Toward the end of my third rattling sequence, I'll start breaking that pile of branches I'd gathered. I'll bust them across my knees, on trees, on one another, on the ground, anywhere that makes loud noise and mimics a real fight. Simply set down the rattle bag, grab the sticks and start breaking them. At this point, I'm on my knees and I start kicking the ground with the toes of my boots. The idea here is to simulate the sounds of deer hooves treading on the ground during a fight. I'll also kick the ground with aggression while rattling. I'll get more aggressive further in the sequence, in order to both increase my volume to reach deer that may not yet have heard me, and to emulate a natural fight.

At the end of that third sequence, or maybe the fourth, depending on how I feel, I'll pound the ground a couple times with the club I

167

picked up. Often, when bucks battle, other deer gather on the periphery and watch the fight. Several times I've watched does and young bucks stomp a front foot, ears perked, body alert. I'm not sure why they do this. Perhaps it's to send a warning sound to other deer in the area. Maybe it's to disperse sent on the ground from their interdigital glands. But whatever the reason, I know it's loud. Any sound traveling through a solid surface, in this case the ground, carries a long way.

By using the stick and pounding it on the ground, I know I've caused bucks to come in that otherwise may not have. Once late in the archery season, I rattled in a buck and used the club to help bring him in. He was a little three point, and too small to shoot. The next evening I was back out in the woods and watched a buck working a trail. His nose was tight to the ground and I could see he was a nice buck. The first sound I made was with the club beating the ground. I hit the ground twice. He twisted his head, glared uphill into the dark shadows in which I sat, and came on a trot. I arrowed that deer, a 126-inch buck, inside 25 yards. A few years prior I killed a big buck with the same approach, no rattling or grunts, just pounding the ground.

Now, back to the rattling sequence… After the third sequence, where I've rattled aggressively, busted branches and pounded the ground, I'll wait for about five minutes before making a sound. If I know deer are within earshot, I might wait as long as 10 minutes to see if something shows up. After that, if nothing appears, I'll repeat the same aggressive sequence, complete with busting sticks and ground pounding. This time I'll rake a tree or some brush and maybe include a couple of deep grunts.

Blacktail bucks, at least the bucks I've hunted and observed, are not very vocal when compared to whitetails, so I keep my grunting to a minimum. Also, personally, I've never observed a fighting buck make grunts. The only bucks I've seen grunt were ones that were actually chasing does, or just got done lip-curling and likely loved what they smelled.

With those thoughts in mind, I'll grunt to get the attention of bucks, but my reasoning is to do it from a non-fighting buck's point of view. More than likely this would be from a buck that came to watch the fight, and then decided to steal a doe. This often happens, where the biggest buck gets so caught up in fighting, that he neglects his does, while another buck comes in and kidnaps them.

Following that last aggressive sequence, I'll silently wait again for as long as ten minutes, though usually closer to five or six minutes. From there on out, I'm maintaining an aggressive sequence, complete with rattles, grunts, some doe bleats, breaking branches, raking trees and pounding the ground. When I'm done rattling in an area, I'm hot, sweaty and tired. It's not a passive tactic by any means and when I leave, it looks like a rototiller has mangled the land.

On average, I'll remain in one place for about 45 minutes to an hour when rattling during the late season, sometimes more, sometimes less. Again, it all depends on the situation, the weather, wind currents and direction, how the deer seem to be moving over the past couple of days, and more. I don't have one set plan that I stick to. Deer and their environment are in perpetual change this time of year, and how they act one day may differ from how they act the next. Their behaviors may even change from morning to evening.

One thing I will do when given the opportunity, is combine doe bleats and grunts, usually without any rattling involved. Preferably, this is done when I see bucks chasing does and want to pull them away. I don't wan to risk spooking them with a mock fight, so I go about capturing their attention in a more subtle manner. My approach is based on natural behavior. The times I've heard bucks grunt and does bleat are when they're playing chase, not when bucks are fighting. Several times I've pulled bucks off does that were not yet in heat, and brought in single bucks that were out cruising, by using nothing more than a doe bleat and maybe a grunt or two. I've found this to work best on migratory bucks, which can be very aggressive this time of year. It's also worked well on foothill bucks, I think due to the propensity for so many other bucks to move into their area this time of year.

When combining grunts and bleats, I like being able to spot a deer first so I can observe their reaction to the sounds. This is because if a buck is on a hot doe, there's virtually no chance of pulling him away. It's also due to the fact the terrain is so brushy, I don't want to waste time cold calling, or calling to deer I cannot see, for even if they do hear me, there's no guarantee they'll come in. Calling sends a totally different message than rattling and the sounds don't carry as far as rattling. Whether calling or rattling, there are never any guarantees.

One point worth noting, in all my years of hunting, I've personally never heard or observed a doe making an estrous bleat. While several call companies advertise a doe-in-estrous call, I have yet to hear it actually occur in the woods, nor have I talked with anyone who has. Why then, do such calls work? I think it simulates more of a fawn distress call, something I've heard a great deal of in the woods. This sound will get the attention of bucks, for they likely figure that if a distressed fawn is around, a doe won't be far.

As the season progresses into the post-rut, I'll become less aggressive in my rattling sequences. This is because the bucks, themselves, are involved in less combat. Rather than seeking out other bucks to do battle with and establish dominance, the bucks are back to cruising the land and searching for does that were missed in the first estrus cycle. At this point the bucks have little to prove to other bucks, as their primary goal is to service a stray doe here and there.

Because does are on a 28 day cycle, the post-rut can drag on for a long time, depending on when the initial rut timing occurred in your hunting area and how many does were not bred at that time. Typically, the post rut can commence as early as mid-November, or run as late as toward the end of December. Most of the post-rut behavior I've observed has been early to mid-December, in the areas I have hunted for years. Thanksgiving time is also a time of heightened post-rut movement.

Because the behavior of bucks has become less aggressive than when they were in the pre-rut and peak rut, the rattling I do this time of year is usually less aggressive. I've brought in many bucks this time of season while simply pounding that club on the ground. Again, I think this is a warning signal blacktails use to communicate, but it also draws deer in by piquing their curiosity.

When I do rattle, it's more with the approach of what I use during the pre-rut. One thing I will do a bit more is make rubs. The sound of antlers thrashing small trees and brush, rather than other bucks, also seems to capture the interest of nearby bucks. I believe the act of beating brush is something that's a bit less intimidating, for the simple message being sent is that of marking a territory in order to communicate the fact that there's an available buck in the area. Both bucks and does will recognize the rubs as new when they see and smell them, and

170

hopefully a buck will actually hear them being made and come to investigate.

If I know a buck is in the area and he's not responded to my calling and rub making, I'll try and go back into the same area two to three days later and try it again. I did this one season, where I set up, rattled and rubbed on some small trees with vigor. Though no buck came in that day, I returned three days later to find a series of rubs near mine. Feeling confident the buck was still in the area, I kept at the rattling and making rubs. It worked, and a 117-inch buck soon came to investigate. My arrow found it's mark and the deer went less than 50 yards before expiring.

During the time of pre-rut is when bucks start making rubs. The intensity and frequency increases as the rut peaks, then it wanes as the post-rut comes and goes.

I'm often asked two questions about blacktails and rubs. One, do they make rub lines, and two, do they make scrapes? My answer to both is, sometimes. In all my years of hunting blacktails, I've still not figured out the frequency and consistency of when, where and why bucks lay down scrapes or make rub lines. I've seen both, and all I can say is I still have a lot to learn about each of them.

Some of the most impressive rub lines I've seen have been at about the 3,000 to 3,500 foot elevation point, where bucks have rubbed multiple trees usually following the path of an old, grown-over skid road or fairly open bench. I've seen lots of rubs in a small area in the foothill, valley floor and open country habitats of blacktails. From what I've seen of rubs in these areas, they've been random rather than lain out in a well defined line commonly associated with the whitetail's practices. I'm convinced that in several of the areas where I've observed such patches of rubs, they are often made by more than one buck.

As for scrapes, I have seen some, though I've never actually watched a buck making a scrape. The ones I've found have been along the valley floor, usually under willows lining defined trails. I've never seen multiple scrapes put down in a defined trail like whitetails do, rather rudimentary scrapes here and there. Some tracks I have seen inside of these scrapes have been wide, leading me to conclude that they were made by mature bucks. Again, I have a lot to learn about blacktail rub lines and scrapes, but that's the beauty of blacktails, there's always so much to learn.

When I do find rub lines, or a series of rubs in a small area, the next clue I look for is nearby does. The rubs confirm buck are, or were, in the area, and the presence of does means there's hope of a buck still being in the area to pick up females that weren't bred in the first go around. If there are no does around, I'll rattle and make some mock rubs near the buck's rubs in an attempt to lure him in. If he doesn't respond within 20 minutes or so, I move on. One thing I've found during my post-rut calling experiences, are bucks responding fairly quickly. I think this is because competition among bucks is less; therefore they are quicker to react to another buck being in their territory.

If nothing responds to the first rattling setup, I'll move to another area where rubs are and call again. If nothing comes in, then I'll go searching for does. Chances are if the buck hasn't responded to rattling near his area of rubs, he's out looking for does. Keep in mind, bucks won't usually travel as far in the post rut to find does as they did in the pre-rut. Their bodies are telling them the end of the breeding season is near and as a result they start feeding and sticking more closely to their core area. But they will be looking for hot does within their territories.

Once does are located, I'll do more calling with doe bleats and grunts than I will with rattling. The idea is to simulate a receptive doe and a buck chasing a doe. This is less threatening than rattling, breaking sticks and rubbing trees, and has worked well for me in post-rut hunts. When I do rattle late in the season, I'm careful not

Using doe bleats, Daren Henderson brought this massive Cascade blacktail into bow range, then made good on the shot.

172

to overdo it, whereby risk spooking a buck out of the area with too much aggressive antler-clashing.

How I decide to go about rattling and calling in the late season depends on how the deer are behaving. Pay close attention to the clues deer are leaving, how they're acting, how far and where they're moving, and what impact hunting pressure and weather conditions may be having on them.

One thing I do suggest is, any time a fresh snow falls, get out and hunt or at least scout. You can scout by rattling and calling, and picking up deer movement with snow on the ground is easier than when the habitat is brown and all looks the same. It's a very good way to see what's out there.

Even if you've filled your tag and won't be hunting until next season, it's rare that snow falls in some of the low-elevation habitats where most blacktails live. When a snow falls, make it a point to get into the field and see what's happening with the deer. You'll be able to see sign you otherwise would not be able to detect, and what you'll learn can open your eyes to just how many deer are out there, and how and when they're moving.

Look to see which trails they are using to access feeding and bedding areas. Find where their bedding areas are. One thing that will surprise you is how many times a deer will bed, get up, walk, feed and re-bed during the course of the day. Big bucks won't do this as much as does, but you'll be surprised at how much movement there is late in the season. The movements may not cover much ground, but the fact the deer are up and utilize several beds should tell you something. These are key clues to learning where to call and rattle from.

As the season progresses, search for big bucks closer to their core areas. Trophy bucks restrict their movement to small areas fairly quickly. Their goal is to take in needed calories, and more importantly not expend energy. If there are does to inspect, they'll do it, but they won't spend as much time and energy as they did a week or two prior. This late in the year, food carries little nutritional value and the deer know it. They will not waste much effort searching for food if their energy output exceeds the input. This all means that concentrating efforts in core territories is important.

The later in the year the late season progresses, the more challenging it becomes for hunters to learn from the deer themselves simply because they are more reclusive. But there is a lot to be learned this time of year. If you hunt migratory deer in the high country earlier in the season, it is fun spending time in their wintering grounds to see what bucks are around. While doing so rattling and calling them can be a productive learning tool. Then you know what caliber of bucks you'll be looking for next season in the higher elevations.

No matter when you hunt, the late season can be a great time to get in the woods, rattle, call, and see what bucks are out there. If you hold a late season tag, it's even better, for many big bucks are taken this time of year. I've arrowed some of my best bucks in December, and I've discovered many bucks I didn't know were around at this time. Bottom line, the late season, all the way to the end, is a good time to be afield, learning all you can about these elusive deer.

Scent Use & Control

Because the late season is a time when most bowhunters are in the field, this is also the best time to talk about the use of scents as well as human scent control. Scent control products are one of the fastest growing, and biggest selling, products in the big game hunting world. Making my living from the outdoors, I'm always surprised at what sells in this industry and what doesn't. Some of the best products ever invented hardly sell simply because they're not marketed. Then there are poor performance products selling because they are marketed well. Remember, many products on the market are created to catch the eyes of hunters, not the animals we pursue.

The use of human scent control agents are one of those things that boils down to personal preference. Some folks won't step into the woods without them, others don't care. My take on it is, if it gives you confidence and you believe in it, by all means, use it.

Personally, I use scent control products when I'm going to be sitting in a tree stand or in a ground blind. I'll spray down my boots, lower body and call it good. My goal is to try and mask my scent while I'm traveling to where I'll be hunting. This is because I'll usually have to cross a trail or two that approaching deer may cross, and my hope is that they will not smell where I've been.

I'm not a scent blocking fanatic for the simple reason deer have such a good sense of smell. I've read various reports on how good deer can smell, and am not sure which are correct, if any. One report said deer can smell 3,000 times better than a human. Another report said a deer's nose is 1,100 times superior to a dog's.

No matter how strong a deer's sniffer, there's no doubting it is well above what humans can even fathom. Interestingly, in the world of mammals, humans have a very, very poor sense of smell. I guess we should be thankful for this.

So, do scent prevention methods really work? Personally, I've tried much of what's on the market, and given my hunting style, I find it most productive to simply not give my scent away by foolishly hunting with the wind. I don't wash my clothes in any special detergents. I don't hang them in separate closets, store them in plastic tubs, hang them outside of camp or change into them once I reach my hunting grounds. I don't spray myself down from head-to-toe with an entire bottle of scent blocking spray during the course of a day's hunt. I don't chew special gum, wash my hair with special soap or use special deodorants when I'm hunting on the move. Here's why.

Because a deer's sense of smell is so good, you'd virtually have to seal yourself inside a plastic bag in order to not be smelled. Even if you do use scent blocking agents, human odor is still mixing with them and can be detected. But if you play the wind, always hunting into or across it, your scent won't be carried to an animal, no matter how bad you may smell. Keep in mind, rarely do I go on a blacktail hunt where I'm not sweating within minutes of the hunt. Sweat means smell, and there's no way to contain these foul odors all of the time.

Since a great deal of human odor is excreted from our heads and hands, largely through sweating, I'm not one for trying to cover that up when I want my body to breath. Most of our body heat escapes through our head, and I don't want to retard that when I'm actively hunting. I want to stay comfortable while hiking and this can only be achieved by letting our bodies breathe. That's why I like wearing hunting clothes that let my body heat escape.

At the time of this writing, there's no true breathable, stretchable waterproof clothing on the market. This is why I carry a thin set of rainwear, so I can put it on as needed over the outside of my breathable, stretchable hunting clothes. The same is true for scent blocking clothes; their purpose is to keep your smell inside, whereby not allowing your body to breath. That's fine if you're sitting, but not many blacktail hunters sit.

When hunting from stands, I will use some scent blocking agents that help me get into the stand without leaving too much human odor behind. But I won't give up the wind. If the wind is not right, I won't sit in that stand. A deer's nose is simply too good. But what about all those whitetail shows, where bucks walk underneath a stand from down wind? Remember, air travels in layers, like water, and chances are, the wind is simply carrying over the buck's head, at least that's the idea behind hanging tree stands high in trees. Then again, even a little bit of scent blocking coverage can make a difference. That's why I will use some of these products when hunting from stands or blinds.

What scent blocking agents you use and how religiously you use them comes down to personal preference. I know of several private land blacktail hunters who nail record book bucks virtually every year, and they credit much of their success to scent blockers. I also know of guys who hunt bigger country, take giant bucks with regularity, and don't use a drop of it.

Experiment around and see if there's something in the form of scent blocking agents that you like. If you do, great, stick with it. But whatever you do, don't intentionally give your wind away. Hunting into the wind is easier said than done, for air currents are in constant change, not to mention the fact animals don't always show up where expected. There are many uncertainties in hunting, and wind carrying scent molecules tops the list.

If hunting from a stand or blind, approach them from downwind. This will ensure that animals approaching from upwind won't smell you, even if you have rubbed on some bushes, grass or tree branches. Wearing rubber boots and spraying the lower body with scent eliminator is a good idea in such situations.

As for clothes designed to capture human odor, like carbon suits, I don't have much confidence in them when hunting on the ground. Human scent levels overpower the blocking capability of the clothes, meaning animals will smell you. In fact, I think such garments can hurt, for hunters get careless and believe the suits will do more than what they are capable of. Then again, if you can sit in a stand, free of perspiration, such scent blocking clothing only needs to work good enough to convince a buck to stick around for an extra second or two, whereby allowing you to get a shot.

When it comes to scent-free soaps, shampoos, laundry detergent, gum, breath mints and other such odor-reducing agents, I say use them if they give you added confidence. Just be careful not to give away the wind too often, for you only get so many chances during the course of a season. Keep in mind that a buck may second-guess what he sees or hears, but never questions what he smells.

Growing up I started running my own trap line in fourth grade. I trapped fox, coyote, bobcat, raccoons and more. When I moved to Alaska, I ran extensive lines for wolves, wolverine, lynx and fox. During my trapping years, my number one objective was to eliminate human scent. If the human odors weren't gone, the animals wouldn't come in. I did this by wearing rubber gloves and rubber boots, and also boiling my traps. I didn't want any human odor on the traps, or around my sets, period.

Hunting is different than trapping, because we can't leave the area, meaning our scent lingers. The best approaches I've found for cutting down on human scent are wearing rubber boots and spraying down my lower body with scent-eliminating spray, whereby allowing me to access stands and blinds.

Drippers with fresh doe urine can be very effective at attracting and stopping big bucks.

If you ask me about the use of deer scents to attract bucks, that's a different story. This is something I've experimented with a bit, but not as much as I should have. When I've used them, it's been nothing more than doe-in-heat urine to help stop bucks along trails. From what little I've played with, I'm a firm believer that they do work. I took one of my best bucks with the aid of multiple urine drips.

The key to any scents, especially urine drips, are to catch the attention of bucks, bring them in and stop them for a shot. When bucks stop and smell urine on the ground this time of year, they are analyzing it through the vomeronasal organ, which is located on the roof of the mouth, and serves some functions similar to that of the nose. Its primary function is thought to be that of analyzing urine in order to help synchronize the breeding readiness between the does and bucks. The idea is to make sure both bucks and does are in top breading condition at the same time, to pass along superior genetics and maximize overall herd survival rates.

When you see a buck sniffing urine, then lifting his head, curling his upper lip and sniffing the air, this is called the Flehmen gesture. The buck will also take air into his mouth so that the scent makes contact with the vomeronasal organ. When you see a buck repeatedly lip curling like this, and he's trailing a doe, chances are she's in estrous. Getting bucks to stop and sniff a scent drip can be very effective this time of year.

Hunting buddy, John Costello, is more versed on scent use than I am; in fact, he's experimented more with scents for blacktail hunting than anyone I know. Here's what he has to say.

"I don't start using attractant scents until November," shares Costello. "I do use deer cover scents in the early season, to help mask human odors, but haven't had any luck using attractants until the late season, during the migration and the rut."

Costello does a great deal with blacktail scrapes and scent applications. "Starting in early November I'll make mock scrapes and use buck urine in them," he shares. "I make my own scrapes but I also add to existing scrapes that I find in the woods."

It took Costello a long time to figure out how to look for blacktail scrapes, as they're not as evident as those made by whitetails. He looks for rubs along ridgelines, travel corridors and in brushy draws, where bucks spend a lot of their time during November. Often times, a series of rubs lead to scrapes, which make it convenient for does to find bucks. "It's almost like a place where they meet for a social gathering," observes Costello.

Costello has been surprised with the size of some of the scrapes he's found over the years. "Some scrapes are very large, which indicates several deer will use them. These large scrapes are used year after year, too."

On the other hand, Costello admits some scrapes are not that easy to locate. "Some scrapes are hard to find, looking more like deer beds than actual scrapes. One of the keys I look for is that of a branch or a limb hanging over the scrape. This is the branch bucks use to rub their scent glands on."

Costello spends much of his time hunting the foothills of southern Oregon's Cascade Range. Here he focuses on both resident and migratory bucks. What he's concluded over his years of studying scrapes is that they are usually strung out in a line, rather than a random one found here and there.

"Once I find some scrapes, my goal is to keep them fresh," points out Costello. "During the rainy times, scrapes can age quickly, and I do my best to keep them active in hopes of keeping the does, and more bucks, coming to them."

When freshening up scrapes with buck urine, Costello uses a variety of brands. His mindset is to simulate different bucks using the scrape. From early November, to the time when the rut gets closer, Costello primarily uses buck urine.

As the rut approaches, Costello switches from buck urine to doe-in-heat scents, which he'll put in the scrapes as well as hang on wicks in strategic locations. When applying these scents, he wears rubber gloves and rubber boots, to help cut down on contaminating the area with human odors.

"I only use the wicks when hunting from stands or ground blinds," Costello shares. "I'll hang the wicks along trails, as well as just off the trail, where I want to get bucks to stop for a perfect shot angle. I keep adding scent to the trails I hunt throughout the course of the season, and no question, this has forced deer to actually shift their trail use from the ones they used to use, to the one that is now heavy in scent I've applied."

Reflecting back on the section of this book where scent glands and communication were covered, Costello's approach and what he's found makes perfect sense. When exiting an area for the day, Costello will leave the wicks hanging, so the scent will continue to be distributed, letting deer know there is action in the area. This helps keep deer around for when he returns.

Costello, and hunters I've talked with who use estrous doe scents for blacktails, share the same sentiment, in that not all scents work. Be sure to get fresh urine which comes from a single doe, not a blend of does. This pure urine is more expensive than the blends, but is worth it. Look for expiration dates, and use only fresh urine.

There are some blacktail scents on the market, but from what I've learned, both from my own trial and error, and from fellow hunters, some of the whitetail scents work great, maybe even better. It could be due the technology behind the capturing of these pure scents, or how they are handled and processed. Even though they come from whitetails, blacktails don't seem to mind.

When hanging doe-in-heat scents from a wick, monitor which direction the winds are coming from, keeping in mind deer usually move into the wind. Costello demonstrated this perfectly the first time I hunted with him. It was mid-November, and the rut was in full-swing. Before hopping into my blind, Costello hung four different wicks around the area. Each one was strategically placed to not only catch the attention of bucks, but to pull them into perfect shooting position. It worked. Before I arrowed a mid-130-inch buck, I could have taken a half-dozen others, three of which were Pope & Young animals. Every one of them checked out the estrous scent dripping from the wicks.

When it comes to human scent elimination, and attracting bucks through the use of deer scents, there is still much to be learned. Ever-changing technologies will continue impacting our approach to hunting, no doubt. Find what gives you the most confidence and hunt smart, for while technology changes, wind directions and a buck's sense of smell don't.

Decoy Use

My indoctrination to using decoys on blacktail deer was a humbling one, yet proved they do work. I packed in a lifesize 3D target – a medium sized whitetail buck – into my hunting area and erected it 20 yards from my ground blind. That evening I called and rattled, but didn't see a thing.

Rather than pack the decoy out, I left it standing overnight and returned at first light to give it another try. I'd seen a couple good bucks in the area, and picked up even more activity on trail cameras, so was confident there were good animals in the area. But when I walked up on my decoy, I discovered it became the target for another buck.

My 3D target had been torn apart and was laying in six pieces, scattered all over the ground. The number of antler gouges in the foam body was impressive, but not nearly as eye-opening as the amount of blood left on the target's backside from the rampaging buck. The entire rump was covered in blood, while hoof marks dug several inches deep in the soft ground directly behind the hind legs. It appeared that the challenging buck spent a good deal of time trying to mount the decoy, then grew frustrated and tore it apart. I never did kill a buck there that season, but learned decoys will attract bucks.

As with any hunting tactic, timing is important when employing decoys. Decoys are most effective during the pre-rut, rut and post-rut periods. One word of caution on decoy use: Never carry them in to public land hunting grounds while any rifle seasons are open. The reasons are obvious.

There are several brands of decoys on the market, and while most hunters prefer painting the bodies, faces, legs and tails to look more like blacktails, whitetail decoys will work. The hardest part for blacktail hunters is carrying the bulky decoys into the often hard to access hunting area. If you can, pack them in a few days early and stuff them in the brush. Then, when you arrive to hunt, all you have to do is set them up.

During the pre-rut, try placing one or two young buck decoys facing each other, a few yards apart. Add a doe decoy for realism, and even a fawn decoy, since fawns are still hanging with mom this time of year.

During peak rut, try using a single buck decoy situated behind a pair of does with a fawn off to the side. This gives the real appearance that a buck is after a hot doe, and junior is still tagging along.

For post-rut decoying, try placing a buck behind a single doe, with no fawn decoy. This presentation sends the message that there is a hot doe that was missed being bred during her first estrous cycle.

The use of doe in heat scents, as well as buck scents, only adds to the realism of a decoy setup. Many hunters choose to douse the decoys with odor-eliminating sprays, and then apply the scents to surrounding vegetation. Place the buck scents by the back legs of the buck decoy, and the doe scents near the hind end of the doe decoys.

Rattling and calling, be it from a blind or tree stand, are important when it comes to capturing the attention of bucks. This is especially true when hunting in thick cover, where a deer might not be able to see the decoys. Once a buck starts coming in, limit the amount of rattling and calling you do, letting the decoys do the work.

If hunting lowland blacktails where turkey populations thrive, adding a couple turkey decoys can help add realism to the set. These confidence decoys can make a difference.

Keep in mind that, as with all hunting methods, nothing is 100% effective, not even decoying. But I'm confident that as more blacktail hunters turn to using decoys, they'll be kicking themselves for not doing so sooner. It takes time and effort, but once you fool a trophy class buck, you'll become a decoy believer.

Stands & Blinds

Late season tree stand and ground blind hunts can be very effective, especially for archers. Much of what was touched on earlier in regards to stand and blind placement, applies here. But there are some specific points to keep in mind that correlate stand and blind placement with deer behaviors this time of year.

If hunting migratory deer, remember that they'll keep dropping in elevation as the season progresses. I've heard of more than one late season hunter who packed a tree stand into the Cascades and hunted from it all day without seeing a single deer, only to discover the deer had already moved out of the area, or hadn't begun migrating yet.

Likewise, if hunting close to or within the wintering grounds, remember that a constant influx of deer means herd dynamics are always changing. This also means, depending on doe populations, that several bucks may concentrate in a single area. Be careful not to put stands or blinds in the core area where does bed or even feed, rather along the travel routes that get them there. This will ensure a less invasive approach for hunters. If you do set up where does feed, do so along brushy fringes to help hide you.

Only in certain situations will a blind or stand be placed near a food source, and this decision will be up to the hunter. The food plots and natural food plantings that we touched on earlier in the book are prime examples of where it's okay to situate stands near food sources. The same is true for hunting over mineral supplements. If does are conditioned to come in to a consistent food source, there's a very high likelihood bucks will follow. These are great places to set up blinds and hang stands, where legal.

If hunting resident deer, try and situate stands and blinds near travel routes. Preferably, the more travel routes that connect with one another, the better the chances of finding deer. This is the only time of year where I'll actually set blinds and stands along primary travel routes, even though bucks don't normally use them. The reason I do this is because in the late season, a buck's primary concern is finding estrous does, and to do this, he has to smell where they've been. Since most does travel along main trails, it only makes sense that bucks will do the same.

Keep in mind that bucks aren't using these trails to travel long distances, simply to hop on them and see what messages may have been left by does. This means bucks will likely inspect these trails where most does travel along them, namely near the entry or exit point leading into or out of brushy cover. Be careful not to position your setup too far out in the open, for a big buck might not come that far into a clearing.

Remember, most big bucks rarely use primary trails, even during the rut. But this doesn't mean they won't inspect them for does, doe urine or scents left behind from various glands of does. The key is for hunters to situate their stands near places along trails that show heavy doe movement, for the bucks will visit them.

This time of year, scouting and using trail cameras can lend a great deal of direction when it comes to figuring out where to hang stands or erect blinds. Look for signs of increased deer activity and pockets of does, and then go from there. Keep an eye out for tracks that splay wide and dig deep into the dirt, for this is a good sign that a rutting buck is in the area. Look for fresh rubs, urine spots on the ground and anything else that tells you deer are using the area.

When you put all the pieces of the information puzzle together, you'll be better prepared for figuring out where to place your stands and blinds. Proper placement of these hunting tools is the key to success, for if they're not in the right place, you won't see deer. Study, think and make logical decisions based on what information you've gathered, then be patient. When it all comes together, it's a great feeling of accomplishment knowing you outwitted a trophy blacktail on his turf, without him even knowing you were there.

Weather

Late blacktail season and bad weather are synonymous with one another. Sure there are those fair weather days that all hunters smile about this time of year, but for the most part, bad weather is the norm for the late season blacktail hunter.

I can close my eyes and vividly recall the days before I was of hunting age, when Dad and both of my grandfathers would come in from a day in the blacktail woods. Back in the 1960s, the general rifle season ran later than it does today, and hunting during the rut was the norm. I remember them coming in soaking wet, smiles on their faces and the smell of rutting bucks on their clothes. For them, the more extreme the weather, the better they liked it.

Today, my mindset is much the same. Give me some bad weather and I can just about guarantee the chances of tagging a big buck will increase. This time of year more than any other, bad weather seems to have little effect on buck behavior, in fact, I believe foul weather gets big bucks fired-up even more. This could be because the cool temperatures associated with rain and snow allows a buck's body temperature to stay cooler, meaning he can be more active without overheating. It could also be due to the fact more scent from the does is being left on the ground and hanging low in the heavy, humid air.

I don't know how many times over the years I've watched big bucks aggressively pursue does in a driving rain. On several occasions I've seen record book bucks follow herds of does and patiently lay in wait for them to slip into heat. These weren't little rain showers the bucks bedded in, rather torrential downpours that were so intense, it was tough keeping track of the deer through my spotting scope.

I'm convinced that when the hormones of bucks are in full production, they simply are not impacted by bad weather. It's likely due to

184

the fact these deer live in such a mild climate, overall. Really, weather conditions are not too rigorous for blacktails, other than for those living at high elevations where seasonal snow falls.

In habitats where snow does fall, the deer adapt by simply migrating. Some migrations are early, before the snow falls, others take place after a considerable amount of snow has blanketed the ground. When, exactly, a high country buck or Cascade blacktail decides to migrate, I believe, is based more on food availability and photoperiods than bad weather. California high country bucks, for example, are known for their early season migrations which commence well before any snow falls. Their early movement is likely due to a lack of quality food. Cascade bucks, on the other hand, may tolerate more than a foot of snow before dropping in elevation because they have so much food available to them.

When rains and snows fall, don't hesitate to head into the field. These conditions are my absolute favorite to hunt in for the simple fact deer are on the move and the forest floor is quiet. These two factors make the chances of sneaking up on a big buck better than normal.

The only time I've seen big bucks restrict their movement and aggression during the late season is in extremely cold rains combined with harsh winds. Freezing rain, wet snows and even hard rains can all turn very cold, even for deer, when you throw in 40 mile per hour winds. On days when the wind-chill takes the mercury low, big buck movement will slow. Just how low of temperatures they will tolerate comes down to the deer themselves. From what I've observed, the farther south a deer lives, the more sensitive they are to cold, wet conditions, thus their movements slow down sooner than a buck living farther north.

When bad weather hits your hunting area, make it a point to be in the woods, for the chance of spotting a trophy buck will increase. Take your waterproof spotting scope and binoculars and spend serious time covering ground with your eyes. If hunting in brushy habitat, be prepared to cover ground on foot. This is the time for hunters to be aggressive. With the conditions being so wet and having predictable winds to work with, there's no better opportunity to slip up close on a trophy buck.

Does, Does, Does

While I put a good deal of time in to watching does on a year-round basis, the culmination of those efforts comes together in the late season. All the off-season scouting, searching for does, and mapping where they're located, boils down to these last two months of the year, when the pre-rut, peak rut and post rut all unfold.

Find the does and keep track of them, for bucks will not be far. This time of year, does are the most important influence over buck behavior. Why a buck behaves in a certain way usually correlates with what's happening with the does in his area at this particular time of year. Whether a buck is cruising the land in the pre-rut in search of receptive does, locked up with a group of does in the peak of the rut or looking for stragglers in the post rut period, their behavior is dominated by the does.

The urge to pass along their genes is so strong, bucks will quit eating, endure what can be fatal battles, tolerate sleep deprivation, and

Monitoring does is one of the best late-season
approaches there is when it comes to finding big bucks.

186

put their bodies as well as minds through various forms of stress unlike anything they experience during any other time of the year. Establishing dominance and breeding with does is the primary focus in a buck's life.

Because bucks are so dedicated to breeding does and reaching as high in the pecking order as possible, their behaviors center around where does go and what they do. If does are up feeding, bucks will become especially aggressive in their search for estrous does. The more active does are, the more they urinate, and bucks will try and check each urine spot to determine a doe's state of estrous. Bucks may stick with a herd and continually circle them, sniffing the ground and does' genitals, or they might bounce from doe herd to doe herd, checking their status. This time can be a real juggling act for bucks and hunters, alike. For hunters, patience and persistence are critical.

If does bed down for the day, bucks may stick close to them or move off in search of other does. What I've observed is if does bed down and bucks bed down with them, there is a doe that's in heat or very close to being in heat. Because of this, the buck won't leave the group of does for fear of missing out or risk having another buck slip in while he's gone. If does bed down and a buck moves away from them, it's usually because he has other does in the area to check on to see if they've reached breeding status. These two scenarios – whether a buck moves or stays with does – show the important roles does can play in helping hunters find bucks in the late season. The key is keeping track of the does and monitoring them closely this time of year.

Because bucks can move around, and because so many bucks come out of hiding this time of year, it's best to locate as many doe herds as possible and continually check their whereabouts. If does move, it likely won't be far, unless, of course, they are migratory does. But even if they are migratory does, these can be the best of all to follow since they move in through open timber, meaning bucks must follow. These Cascade bucks are some of the most exciting to hunt this time of year, and there can be many of them which converge on groups of does at any one time. If migrations are taking place at night, during the rutting period, find groups of does and stick with them throughout the day, applying what hunting strategies will best fit the situation.

If monitoring resident does, watch them during the entire rut, for bucks can move in at any moment. As the season progresses, locate bigger groups of does to focus your efforts on. Often, among large groups of does, one or two miss being bred in the time of first estrous, meaning the second go around will find bucks seeking them out. This is often referred to as the second rut, or post rut, by some hunters. It's by no means as intense as the first rut, and can be spotty, but it's also a great time to close the deal on sex-crazed bucks.

Because the peak rut, or initial rut, can be so intense in places of high buck densities, bucks may get so caught up on fighting and chasing off other bucks, they may miss breeding a doe or two. In areas of low buck densities, a buck may also miss breeding a doe if he's out servicing another group of does in a different valley. The post rut, or second rut, can carry on for over a month, depending on when the initial rut kicked off in a specific hunting area.

In the post rut, even if you see a single doe wondering around, it's worth taking the time to closely inspect her. She may have been missed on the first go around, and a wandering buck might find her. In this case, it's all a matter of being in the right place at the right time.

If you do find nice-sized doe herds and no bucks are on them, keep track of them. Chances are a buck's not far. My favorite time to closely watch resident doe herds are when they are on the move, that is, shifting from feeding to bedding areas, or vise versa. I think their movements not only capture the eye of wondering bucks, but their scent becomes more dispersed, especially when they urinate as they move through and area. This smell will often attract bucks and get them fired-up.

On migratory does, when the rut is peaking or slowing down, it's worth spending an entire day on them. Often the bucks will move in on these herds from behind, or from a side hill angle. Knowing which angle a buck may approach a doe or herd of does allows you to play the wind and setup accordingly. This can be especially important if calling or rattling.

During the late season, don't underestimate the value of does and what they have to offer. Keeping a watchful eye on does can lead you to learning a great deal about deer behavior, and it can lead you to the buck of a lifetime. That's what's so fun about blacktail hunting this time of year; anyone can score on a record book buck at any time. It's one of the most addicting times to hunt, no question.

Mega-Buck Invasion

Earlier I stated the need to avoid delving too deeply into the core area of big bucks, for fear of spooking them. There is an exception to this. I have no scientific data to back this up, and I'm not even sure if it's true 100% of the time, but based on what I've personally seen, and some seasoned hunters I've spoken with over the years have observed, the late season is a time to encroach upon the core area of big bucks.

I believe some of the biggest, oldest blacktail bucks are going over-looked by hunters. This is because the older a buck gets, the harder it becomes for him to survive. If a big buck can live to be seven or eight years old, his focus in life shifts from eating, sleeping and reproducing, to simply surviving.

Old bucks will likely not engage in battle like they used to, if at all, for fear of being injured or even killed. Their core area will also shrink, for at this stage in their life, all they care about is staying alive.

Because the competition among bucks is so aggressive during the rut, and the pressure they receive from hunters throughout their life-time is so intense, a low number of bucks live to a ripe age, what we refer to as beyond their prime. But some do live beyond their prime breeding years, and those that do often withdraw into a reclusive life of secrecy. These are some of the biggest blacktails to be had, yet few are taken.

These old, wise bucks become loners during the late season. They may hang near bachelor bucks in the early season, and rely on them to help sense danger, but in the late season, they don't want to have any-thing to do with these bucks, the same ones who could cause potential injury or death.

To avoid confrontations of battle, escape predators – including man – and lead a lifestyle where their caloric intake is simple to attain and burns very slowly, these big mega-bucks will go into seclusion. Their lives are reduced to eating, sleeping and conserving energy, and they do everything possible to make this happen.

Look at any aging mammal. The older they get, the more seden-tary their lifestyle becomes. This is true of dogs, cats, horses, humans and just about every other mammal on the planet, including deer. A less active life leads to energy conservation, and for bucks, this means sleeping or staying in one small area during daylight hours. They know

189

they're vulnerable to predation, and don't want to risk being seen or smelled. They know when hunters are afield, and go to extremes to not be detected.

The key to scoring on these mega-bucks before their antlers start digressing, or reverting back, is invading their core area. These are bucks that are almost totally nocturnal in their feeding habits and over-all movements. You might only know they exist thanks to trail cameras or catching a glimpse of them in the headlights one night. But they are there.

Once you know a mega-buck is in the area, don't be afraid to in-vade his space. Play the wind, use the terrain to your advantage and be ready at all times. When I'm in a buck's space, I'm locked in, expecting to see him. This is an intense time to hunt, for you can't see the quarry, yet you know it's out there. The mental edge I gain in this situation is the fact that I expect a buck to be there; I don't wish him to be there. By doing this, my mind is mentally geared to execute a shot in a split-second's time. I'm wired and ready, and it works. Don't ever get caught simply going through the motions in these hunting situations, for the moment you let down your guard, things will likely happen.

These big, old bucks are the smartest of the smart, and at this point, their only goal is to stay alive. Scout, study the terrain and the deer populations in your hunting area. Learn what's happening around you, monitor the weather, and then figure out the best way to access these bucks in their bedrooms. Over the years we've killed some dandy bucks this way, in the middle of the day, in their beds. It's a very low percentage approach, but can be done, and if you want one of these old boys, it's sometimes the only option available.

Conclusion

Every accomplished trophy blacktail hunter I know has one thing in common: The fact they are willing to continually learn. I believe it's this mindset that has allowed me to be successful.

I'm not an expert on blacktails and never will be. There's simply too much to learn, and I can't accomplish it all in my lifetime. I'm simply blessed to be able to hunt for a living, which means I get to spend numerous days in the field each year. Due to the demand of producing television shows and magazine articles, I'm also under pressure to consistently find success. I do this through the only way I know how, and that's hard work, keeping a positive attitude and an open mind. Once the learning stops, so does the success.

I've learned a great deal from several generations of accomplished blacktail hunters before me, but the most valuable lessons I've learned have been while spending time in the woods, alone. Most of the time I learn from my mistakes, and believe me, I make many of them. The key is recognizing when this happens and working to improve with each error I make.

As I write these final words, my mind is in motion, for another blacktail season is nearly upon us. I'm addicted to blacktails, I admit it. Once you reach this level, they consume your life. It's what you think about day and night, year-round. For me, the seasons can't come fast enough.

The urge to try new tactics in an effort to score on that buck of a lifetime gets stronger with each passing season. Part of the allure is the unknown, the mystery which surrounds these grand bucks. Part of the allure is knowing that success can come at any moment. And when success is finally found, the passion just runs that much deeper, for there is always a bigger buck to be had the following season. The accomplished trophy blacktail hunter is always happy, but rarely content.

I often hear from fellow hunters, their disgruntled opinions as to why so few TV shows and magazine articles feature blacktails. It's simple. They are too hard to hunt, and many writers and TV crews don't have the time, money or energy it takes to close the deal on a trophy buck. Just take a look at what three of the country's top big game hunters have to say about blacktails on the back cover of this book. They pretty much sum it up.

For me, the search for big blacktails will continue until I can no longer hunt. I've been fortunate to live in and travel through some of the most stunning places on the planet, yet I choose to make my home in Oregon's Willamette Valley. Why? It's where big blacktails live.

As we raise our two sons near where both my wife and I grew up, we want to teach them how to become good, safe, dedicated hunters and sportsmen. I feel this is best accomplished through pursuing the Columbia blacktail deer.

One season I had the honor of reportedly becoming the first person to take the western deer slam in a single season. This included desert mule deer, Rocky Mountain mule deer, Coues deer, Western whitetail, Columbia whitetail, Sitka blacktail and Columbia blacktail. Some of the bucks I took were record book animals, but the smallest and one of the most gratifying was the Columbia blacktail. Why? Because my youngest son, Kazden, who was then four years old, was involved.

The little buck fed out of a clearing, and one shot dropped him on the spot. He was only a spike, but could well be the biggest deer I've ever taken. Kazden didn't care how big the deer's rack was; he just wanted to skin it out with his new hunting knife. His focus and dedication to the task carried over to helping cut and package the entire deer. From that point on, he was hooked on deer hunting.

Passing on the joy and challenges of the hunt to my boys is one of the most important goals in my life. It's my fondest wish that Braxton and Kazden will grow to love blacktails as I have, and continue passing along the heritage of these great deer to their children.